Frank Barrett

Folly Morrison

Vol. II

Frank Barrett

Folly Morrison
Vol. II

ISBN/EAN: 9783337040161

Printed in Europe, USA, Canada, Australia, Japan

Cover: Foto ©ninafisch / pixelio.de

More available books at **www.hansebooks.com**

FOLLY MORRISON.

A Novel.

BY
FRANK BARRETT.

IN THREE VOLUMES.
VOL. II.

LONDON:
RICHARD BENTLEY AND SON,
Publishers in Ordinary to Her Majesty the Queen.
1880.

CONTENTS OF VOL. II.

CHAPTER	PAGE
I. TWO MODELS	1
II. OVERSTEPPING THE LINE OF FRIENDSHIP	12
III. THE MAN PURSUED BY A DEAD HARE	26
IV. A RECOGNITION	38
V. THE FILIAL LOVE OF FOLLY	53
VI. A STRANGE VENGEANCE	63
VII. A CHECK	75
VIII. ROLAND SAYS 'NO'	87
IX. A NEW PROSPECT	104
X. WIT AND WISDOM OF SIR ANDREW AVELING	112
XI. ROLAND'S FLING	127
XII. GOOD NEWS	145
XIII. A PROPOSAL	156
XIV. VANE IS INTRODUCED TO FOLLY	170

Contents.

CHAPTER	PAGE
XV. A KISS	183
XVI. FATHER AND DAUGHTER	190
XVII. ANOTHER LECTURE	207
XVIII. A POINT GAINED	219
XIX. VANE'S PROJECT	229
XX. PREPARING FOR HAPPINESS	243
XXI. CORRESPONDENCE	255
XXII. THE WEDDING OF ROLAND AVELING AND FOLLY MORRISON	262
XXIII. AFTER THE WEDDING	272
XXIV. SIR ANDREW AVELING AND JOHN MORRISON MEET AGAIN	284

FOLLY MORRISON.

CHAPTER I.

TWO MODELS.

THE new burlesque was unanimously praised in all the theatrical critiques. With characteristic inconsistency, the same paper which contained the most laudatory notice of Folly's performance in one column, devoted another to a leader condemning this kind of entertainment, pointing to the success at the Levity as another proof of the vitiated taste of the age which tolerated such an exhibition. The effect of this condemnation was even more powerful than the accompanying eulogy. Every night the theatre was filled to overflowing; money was turned away, the free list suspended, and seats were booked three weeks in advance.

Admirers vied with each other in flattering Folly, and left her little or nothing to desire. Her portrait appeared in several weekly illustrated papers; photographic art, which had already pushed the books of beauty from the field, made a rapid stride in popularity by the means of *cartes de visite* of Folly which filled shop windows in the Strand, Cheapside, and Regent Street. Folly herself could not get near for the crowds of men about her own likeness. A well-known artist hit upon the happy idea of making her the subject of his Academy picture. In his studio Roland Aveling was first introduced to Folly.

It happened in this way. Amadis Garnier, coming to Roland's chambers one morning, said:

'I am going round the studios. Will you come with me?'

'I shall like nothing better,' replied Roland, cheerfully.

He had recovered from his fit of asceticism in these latter days—it was now September—and thrown Buckle aside with the unploughed copies of Ruskin and Harrison.

The two gentlemen took a cab, and, after calling at a couple of studios in Fitzroy Square, proceeded to Highgate.

'If Stipple is not at home, we will go on to Scumble's,' said Garnier.

A neat little hired brougham stood before Stipple's door.

'He has a visitor. Shall we be intruding?' asked Roland.

'Not at all. Stipple and I shared a studio before he made a name, and most of his friends are mine. A capital good fellow, Stipple, who has lost nothing by prosperity.'

They were shown into a reception-room, and the servant took their cards. Presently the door opened and Stipple himself, in a velvet tunic, with his palette on his thumb, entered.

'I am hard at work, and should have refused to see anyone but you,' said he, after exchanging greetings with Garnier, and being introduced to Roland. 'I should have dismissed you also, but my model is good-natured, and permits me to invite you to my studio. Will you come?'

'Certainly,' said Garnier. 'Who is this condescending model?'

'Don't you know?' replied the artist, stopping short as they were crossing the vestibule towards his studio, and dropping his voice. 'I thought all the boys knew of my good fortune. I've got this new beauty to sit to me—Folly.'

As Roland caught the words his hands grew moist, and he felt the blood rush to his face.

Stipple's studio was vastly different to the studios in Fitzroy Square, where the walls owed their tint to the action of time and tobacco smoke, and the floors failed to betray their simplicity of yellow deal by the infrequent application of soap and water to their surface.

Black oak, rich tapestries, Persian carpets, Utrecht velvet, trophies of arms, black iron and polished brass, were here employed to satisfy the æsthetic taste of the artist.

For these accessories Roland had no eyes; his attention was centred upon Folly. The girl sat on a high-backed chair, covered with stamped leather, raised upon a daïs, with the heavy tapestry behind her. She wore the pale blue dress she had chosen for her first entrance in the burlesque, and was seated carelessly on a corner of the chair, nursing her foot. The vivacious young girl in her bright dress formed a striking contrast to the old and sombre surroundings, which accorded well with her own instinctive love of dissimilitude.

The gentlemen bowed, being introduced by Stipple. Folly answered with a nod, and said, with a good-humoured smile :

'I mustn't get down from my perch.'

Roland hated slang ; but these words coming from Folly's lips did not offend his nice ear. Stipple naturally drew near his easel, his visitors following. Garnier criticised with the freedom of an old friend and an admirer, entering at once into the technical details of the work. Roland, after one glance at the portrait, turned his eyes to the original. That pleased Folly. She met his eyes boldly, and gave him a smile all to himself. Roland blushed like a girl, dropped his eyes, then looked again. She had her eyes still on him. Her smooth cheek rounded, her dark eyes lengthened, the corners of her pretty lips curved upwards, and, unclasping her hands from her knee, she held up one finger and beckoned to him.

To leave the side of an artist to whom you have just been introduced without apology, to cross his studio for the purpose of talking to his model, is as bold a breach of etiquette as one may commit; but Folly desired and Roland obeyed. Had he shown a want of courage Folly would never have smiled upon him again, and this history would have ended here.

The great resuts of our life are decided by such trifling events as this. Cannot each one of us point to some most trivial accident which connected our past with our present, but for which our lot might have been happier or sadder, as the case may be?

'You are a good boy to come when I want you,' said Folly, highly delighted to find that all the admiration was not to be lavished on the painter.

'I should obey you if you set me a harder task than that,' answered Roland.

'Don't turn round. Your friend and Stipple are both looking at you with their mouths open. It's capital fun. I don't care to sit here alone while everyone is praising his work. It is all a smudge yet, and if it were finished ever so nice I should think it would be pleasanter to look at me—don't you?'

'A thousand times.'

'How you blush—like a little girl. It suits your fair skin and makes you look pretty.'

'I dislike pretty men. I hope I am not pretty enough to be objectionable.'

'Oh no; I like you. I like everyone who likes me.'

'You can dislike no one, then.'

'Oh yes, I do. Lots of men say they like me, but'—with a little gesture of contempt—'they don't.' Some recent experience was troubling Folly's memory, for, after knitting her brows and looking straight before her as she swung her foot to and fro, she turned her eyes upon Roland, and, looking him straight in the face, said, with quick earnestness: 'If you were to meet me in the street, and your wife was with you, you wouldn't cross the street when you saw me coming, and pretend you didn't see me, would you?'

'By George, I wouldn't!'

'No, I know that by your eyes and your blushes. That's why I like you.'

'But I am not married.'

'Then I like you all the more.'

'Still, I am engaged.'

'You wouldn't be ashamed to introduce me to the woman you are engaged to if we met?'

'No; I wish she were here to admire you as I do. I have told her all about you in my letters.'

'That *is* nice. I don't see why we should not be good friends, you and I. So you told her all about me. I knew you directly you came into the room here. It was you who threw me the bouquet last night?'

'Yes.'

'And the one on Saturday?'

'Yes.'

'Did you tell her that?'

'Well, no; I didn't mention that.'

Roland spoke nervously.

'You do next time you write. And you can tell her we are going to be friends, because I like you, eh?'

Roland consented, though his heart misgave him that he could scarcely tell all that without arousing a feeling of jealousy in Madge.

'Where do you live?'

'My home is in the country; but I am staying in Kensington at present.'

'Is that far from Lambeth?'

'About half-an-hour's ride.'

'Then I'll drive you home in my carriage. I hate travelling by myself.'

'Drop me wherever you like. I can make my way home.'

'Then you're not afraid of offending your friend by not returning with him?'

'I am more afraid of offending you.'

'It will serve him right. He's still poking over that picture. We can have a good talk; can't we? It's a nice long way to Lambeth from here for two people; it's a horrid distance for one. I like talking—don't you?'

'Immensely.'

'I am sorry Lambeth is such a little way. I think we'll go to Kensington first. Wait, I have a notion. Suppose we dine together somewhere; then we needn't separate until we get to the stage-door.'

'A splendid idea! How much longer have you to sit?'

'I have not been here twenty minutes yet. I suppose he will want me to sit an hour. And I must not move, and he can't talk. Oh, it's horrid! I tell you what. We'll go at once. I'm tired of sitting. Come on.'

She rose with a brisk movement and a merry laugh, caught her arm in Roland's, and brought him down to the easel.

'If you please I can't sit any longer, and I am going,' she said to Stipple. 'And I shall take your friend with me,' she added, addressing Garnier; and then, in a tone of far greater concern : " Where did I fling that cloak of mine ?'

Stipple had already come by experience to understand Folly's temper, and having the wisdom to make a virtue of necessity, he turned his present misfortune off with a joke, and assisted Folly to find the lost cloak.

The cloak being found, Folly, impatient of delay, interrupted Roland in the midst of his apology to Garnier. Laying one hand on his arm and the other on his friend's, she said to Roland :

'Now, don't waste time. Do go and see if that brougham's at the door. The driver is generally walking up and down a mile away when he's wanted. And you,' she continued, turning her imploring eyes on Garnier, 'pray give us your assistance. We've found the cloak, but where on earth I kicked my walking-shoes to I can't tell.'

* * * * *

'Now this is just what I like,' said Folly, slipping her hand under Roland's arm, as they sat side by side in the brougham, rattling along the Highgate Road. 'It is so exactly what one did not expect. What is the time ?'

She pulled the trinket from her bosom— as a watch it had for some time ceased to be reliable. It had to be shaken and tapped before it would tick, and then indicated no more than half-past ten.

'That can scarcely be right,' said she. 'I didn't rise till eleven.'

'It is just three.'

'Capital! We have four hours for talk. Pretty watch, isn't it?'

'Charming. That is your name on the back?'

'Yes. It was given me when I left the Garden. I will never part with it. But I wish it was a ring or a pair of ear-rings. It is such a shame to hide the beautiful diamonds.'

'Would you like diamonds for your ears?'

'Yes, if somebody I like gave them to me.'

✻ ✻ ✻ ✻ ✻

Before the end of the week Folly had diamonds in her ears, for which Roland had dipped into the sum of money placed at his disposal by Sir Andrew.

CHAPTER II.

OVERSTEPPING THE LINE OF FRIENDSHIP.

THE first days of October were sultry. Roland, coming from his bedroom, thrust open the windows of his sitting-room, with an impatient exclamation, and went out upon the balcony, where he stood leaning upon the ironwork under the striped sunblind, inhaling what little air was to be had.

He lolled there, looking down upon the quiet street in an abstracted mood, until he was abruptly aroused by the unexpected voice of the servant at his elbow announcing that his breakfast was ready.

Three letters lay on his plate. He took them in his hand and seated himself. One bore the blazoned arms and initials of Sir

Andrew. He laid that on the table. The next was addressed in a cramped feminine hand to 'Mr. Roland Aveling, Esq.'; he smiled, and kept that in his left hand. The third was in the free, well-written hand of Margaret; he laid that gently on his father's, with a little nod as to an old friend.

He opened the letter he had retained in his left hand, and read it :

'Dere Frend,
  'It's all rite. If I'd a-ran upstairs before sayin good-nite, I shouldn't had to send this. Stipple is ingaged to-morer thank evins so we shal be able to go for a drive as you perposed cum as soon as you lik. You can't cum to early for your fectionate frend
        'Folly.

'P.S.—Plese excuse riting and bad pen. —Annie Clip.'

Roland put the letter in his pocket, then he poured out a cup of coffee, buttered a piece of toast, and began breakfast.

When he had fortified himself with a little refreshment he opened Margaret's letter, and nibbling his toast the while, read it.

'Come, that's rather too bad,' said he to himself, laying down the half-read letter to butter another slice of toast, 'to hint that I'm neglectful when I wrote only last week. One can't be writing letters every day in the week; and what can you say when there's no news to tell? I must give you a scolding, my little Madge.'

He ate again, and took up the letter. '"You wrote every day"—ah, I passed that —"only one in eight"—mum—mum—mum. Yes, here's where I left off. "What has become of your infatuation for the wonderful little actress you told us so much about some time since? We see her name still in the newspapers; but you have not mentioned her in your last two letters."' He put the letter down once more to drink his coffee.

'Of course I haven't said anything about her,' thought he. 'I was stupid to say so much. One's object in writing a letter is to give pleasure to the reader; and how could it please one girl to hear praises of another? It would be stupid and unkind, too, to make Madge jealous when there is no cause for jealousy. It's clear enough, by her coldness and a certain kind of restraint in her letter, that she is a little bit touched already. I must be careful for the future.'

At this moment his reflections were interrupted by a knock at the door.

'Come in,' he cried.

The door opened, and Amadis Garnier entered.

'Midday is too late for a young fellow of your age,' said the visitor, shaking Roland's hand. 'I breakfasted four hours ago.'

'Model of virtue! Take a seat—you must need it.'

Roland put the un-read and the half-read letters together in his pocket for perusal at a more convenient season, and made himself pleasant to his visitor, chatting on various subjects in the bright, agreeable manner which had made him a general favourite in all society.

'What are you doing to-day, Amadis?' asked Roland, when he had finished his breakfast, pushing back his chair and putting a cigar between his lips.

'I am free—are you?'

'Not quite; I am going to take Folly for a drive.'

Roland looked straight at Garnier, wondering why so simple an act required so great an effort.

Garnier looked at him with a perplexed contraction of the eyes, as if he were trying to read a complicated riddle, and then shook his head with a doubtful smile.

'What's the matter, Garnier? What are you thinking about. Come, you should conceal nothing from your friend.'

'I will not. I am trying to understand an old face with new features.'

'Don't be mysterious. What is it that perplexes you?'

'This affair with the little actress.'

'What do you want to know? Speak bluntly, or I shall doubt your friendship.'

'Bluntly, then. What are your intentions in that quarter?'

'Intentions!'

'What will you do with her?'

'I don't understand you.'

'You are giving the girl a great deal of attention—you are spending money on her freely. With what object?'

'The same object which you have, I hope, Garnier, in giving me the pleasure of your company.'

'Friendship?'

'Yes.'

Garnier smiled.

'I don't know what you are driving at, Garnier; speak up.'

'When a man dangles about a beautiful girl, dines with her, drives with her, gives her diamonds, and makes himself conspicuous by his attentions, it is generally understood that his attachment is stronger than that of friendship.'

'That is to say, then, that I am generally misunderstood. I assure you that no feeling beyond friendship exists between Folly and me.'

Garnier drew a long sigh, as if of relief, and said:

'I am delighted to hear it. But you must be careful, my dear fellow.'

'On whose account?'

'Your own, of course. The girl needs no protection, that's certain. You must forgive my freedom, but, as an old friend, I feel that I am privileged to speak.'

'"Let the galled jade wince: our withers are unwrung,"' Roland quoted, laughing carelessly. 'Come, tell me what I have to fear from this terrible little maid.'

'That you won't be able to get rid of her when you wish to.'

'There is no probability of my wishing it.'

'You have not relinquished your intention of marrying Miss Vane?'

'Certainly not.'

'There's the difficulty. But for that you might continue this "friendship" with impunity—it would be easy to bring the intimacy to a close by going to the Continent for six months; but with a wife and a home that is impracticable. And you must see, as well as I, that it would be impossible to begin your *ménage* with a *liaison* of that kind existing. You would be subject to perpetual annoyances from Folly, and her importunities would complicate your matrimonial affairs, and make you miserable.'

'Have you anything to add to this?' asked Roland, with forced calmness.

'I have only to say that prudence suggests you should break the intimacy at once. You are involved in a coil which the girl will draw tighter about you every day. Depend upon it, she will never part so easily from you as at the present time. It has gone quite far enough—but, happily, not too far, it delights me to find. I shall be very happy to act as mediator, if you wish it.'

'What would you be good enough to do for me?'

'Buy her off. Arrange the best terms I could, stipulating for final and complete separation.'

Roland threw away his dead cigar with an action implying disgust, and then, turning to his friend, said:

'Garnier, I am surprised that you, who know me so well, and profess friendship for me, should think me capable of entertaining the motives you imply, or of acting upon your suggestions. You lead me unwillingly to suppose that you believe me guilty of some unholy kind of alliance with this girl—cruel to her and Margaret, and dishonourable to myself. I must tell you that you mistake me utterly. It is less surprising that you misunderstand Folly, knowing so little of her, and including her in your general estimate of actresses. I will take the trouble to assure you that I am guiltless of any dishonest intentions, and that the girl with whom I have formed a most innocent attachment has motives as pure as mine.'

'I see nothing dishonest in your attachment; but the girl, Roland—are you sure that she is the charming innocent you are?'

'I will swear it. Not a word on her part or mine has passed which I would conceal from Margaret. I admire her as I might a beautiful garden, on which nothing I spend is ill spent. I supply the wants she is unable to gratify, and she takes my presents as I give them, in the innocent spirit of friendship.'

'And she dines with you, drives with you, takes diamonds from you, bewitches you with her eyes, and all that, in a simple Platonic fashion, eh?'

'It is so, unable as you may be to understand so delicate a sentiment as perfect friendship.' Roland rose from his chair and, stamping his foot angrily, said, 'Garnier, you have insulted me.'

'I am your friend—not an enemy; give me at least credit for kindly intentions in speaking to you on a subject which distresses me.'

'Well, well, you're a good old fellow, I know,' replied Roland, softening in a moment to the gentler tone of his companion; 'but you might have spared me this pain. Don't you see, old man, that the raptures you artists go into over a statue may animate the heart of an ordinary individual in looking upon a lovely living woman, and discovering those beautiful traits of character which a marble at the best can only suggest? No one imputes discreditable feelings and intentions to you when you go into rhapsodies over eighteen inches of a chipped torso. On the contrary, you are credited with all the virtues under the sun for your passion.'

No argument is so convincing to a man as his own, especially if it have the effect of closing the discussion. Garnier gave up the contest with a wave of his hands, merely remarking that the continuance of an intimacy on a Platonic basis must depend on the stoical disposition of both parties. Then he turned the subject, and soon after departed.

Roland threw himself on a couch, and reflected on what had taken place. He repeated his own arguments and added others equally convincing. He went so far as to look into the future—a most unusual proceeding with him—asking himself if that danger really existed which Garnier had hinted at. Was it likely that a new element would arise to change the nature of their intimacy?

'Shall I fall in love with her, or she with me? The notion's absurd. Folly is a mere child—acting and thinking like a child. She could not be so open and unreserved with any idea of that kind in her mind. As for myself, there is no fear. Have I not promised to marry Madge?—and is not that a sufficient guarantee that I will love no one else? Have I ever been false, or failed to carry out my undertakings, even when made in the heat of enthusiasm and to be executed only with great personal inconvenience? I said I would marry her, and I will. If I had been of a fickle disposition I should have fallen in love with Folly before now; and even supposing a change were to take place in our sentiments, should I not instantly withdraw? Garnier's argument is based upon an entirely erroneous supposition, and to yield to it in the slightest degree would be to admit the truth of his unjust imputation against Folly. Hang it all! I am in the right, and I will prove it. The rubbish he talked is not worth another thought.'

Coming to this satisfactory conclusion, he sprang up from the couch, changed his coat, and went off with a light heart to the livery stables for the chaise. His confidence in himself was strengthened by what had passed, and he experienced relief from a sense of uneasiness which had for the past week oppressed his mind. The difficulty in writing to Madge seemed less. He could tell her more about Folly, now that he was assured of the innocence of his feeling for her. He was pleased with himself, and hurried along without a thought of the heat—thinking now only of the pleasure of the drive before him, and of Folly's bright face, and the gladness with which she would welcome him.

It is to be feared that if at that moment simple Margaret had met him face to face, she would have made his spirits fall instead of rise. Perhaps—though he might not acknowledge the fact to his own soul—perhaps there was no one in the whole world whom he would not rather have met than the sweet girl he was pledged to marry.

Happily, or otherwise, he met no one he knew until he caught sight of Folly waiting for him on the steps of the modest dwelling in Lambeth Road.

And so it seems that, whatever his intentions were, Amadis Garnier did more harm than good to the cause he had espoused, first by leading Roland to justify conduct which conscience had already whispered him was wrong, and secondly by prompting him to vindicate his assertions.

How far these assertions would bear vindication may be judged by an incident that occurred in the course of their drive.

They were driving through Richmond Park, Folly holding the pair of greys well in hand and plying the whip every other minute. The excitement of driving, the exhilarating effect of the champagne she had drunk at lunch—the young lady already showed the most appreciative taste for that pleasant wine—heightened her colour and increased the natural gaiety of her spirits; the champagne seemed to sparkle in her eyes, and bubble in her merry laugh. Engaged as she was in the management of her ponies, she perceived that Roland, sitting silently beside her, had fixed his eyes ardently upon her face.

'Do I look very pretty?' she asked, without moving her head.

'I can't tell you how pretty.'

She turned her face and looked into his eyes until he could bear their witchery no longer, and bent his head, twisting his clasped fingers convulsively.

Enjoying this proof of her power, and

amused by Roland's agitation, she bent towards him, whispering :

'Wouldn't you like to kiss me ?'

Roland caught hold of her arm fiercely, and crushed his lips upon her shoulder, for Folly, laughing, had drawn her face away.

Then he sat back in his seat, trembling violently, while Folly coolly drew her ponies back to the centre of the road, from which they had been swerved by Roland's sudden clutch upon her arm.

CHAPTER III.

THE MAN PURSUED BY A DEAD HARE.

AMONGST the crowd waiting on the gallery steps of the Levity Theatre for the doors to open was a man who made himself particularly unpleasant to those about him, not by any objectionable demonstration of an active sort, but by merely standing in their midst in his passive offensiveness.

He was an old man, seemingly over sixty, with a round back, high shoulders, and a drooping head, set not in a line with his spine, but, that he might see, at an angle with it. When he took off his hat to drain off the water that had accumulated in the brim—he had walked some distance through the pouring rain of that October night without the protection of an umbrella—his head was shown in all its ugliness. Apparently his head and face had been shaved some six or seven days. A short white stubble spread over his round skull and down to the nape of his neck, round his lips and under his chin, bristling in the folds of loose skin about his throat. The lower jaw fell, and his pendulous under lip displayed a solitary black tooth standing in his gum. The lids of his eyes were red, and hung heavily over his sunken eyes. Iris and pupil had no distinction; both were a pale neutral patch in the bloodshot, yellow cornea. Their vacancy and the open mouth gave an idiotic expression to his face. A thousand wrinkles puckered the skin above the prominent cheek-bones. It seemed as if the substance of his face had dissolved and dropped into the lower part of his cheeks, which hung swollen from his jaws, and showed, even through the grey stubble of his beard, an unwholesome yellow, such as appears in the faces of workhouse inmates. He had a trick of passing his horny hand down one cheek and up the other, giving to his face a grotesque distortion which was not amusing to look at simply because it was repulsive. Sometimes after this peculiar action he would rest one bent and knotted finger upon his sole remaining tooth, pushing it backwards and forwards in the loose gum. Frequently a hiccough would shake his whole frame, to the jeopardy of his tooth and a small flat bottle of rum in the pocket of his sleeved waistcoat, as was evident by the look of alarm with which he felt first one, then the other, after one of these convulsions.

There was nothing peculiar in his dress; it was such as a stable-help might wear. The warmth of these gallery steps brought out the fine aroma from the sodden garments, and filled the whole flight with an odour of chaff and horse-beans.

When the old man arrived at the entrance it was twenty minutes before the time for the doors to open, and the approach by the stairs was full to the street. Nevertheless he got up to the very barrier before the pay-place without effort. People before him, becoming conscious of the mingled perfumes of the stable and the gin-shop floating over their shoulders, turned about, and catching sight of the imbecile old man loosening his one tooth, made way, and not unwillingly allowed him to go on in front. To take off his hat and rub his bristling crown would win him one step in advance; to pull his face on one side and drive it up on the other took him another step upwards; while a hiccough would carry him onwards over three.

'The police oughtn't to let such an old brute as that into a respectable theayter.'

'Horrid old wretch!'

'Just come from prison.'

'Worse luck—pity they didn't keep him there.'

These observations fell upon the old man's ear as he went onward, and were heard with indifference. It was not new to him to be loathed. In the present case he derived benefit from the repugnance he created. He was rather grateful to the people than angry with them: their remarks all helped to procure him a good place. When he got to the barrier he turned his back upon it and looked down at the crowd through which he had passed with a lateral expansion of his mouth that was intended for a smile. Then he felt his tooth and his bottle seriously, and finding both perfectly safe, he laughed audibly—a queer kind of cackling noise rising from his throat.

'Have you got your money?' asked a man, apprehensive that when the time arrived to pass in this idiot would stop the gangway.

The old man nodded.

'Then get it ready—the doors will open directly, and we don't want to be kept waiting half an hour for you.'

The old man fumbled in his pocket obediently, without relaxing the grasp of his other hand upon the bottle.

'One shilling,' said his adviser, holding up one finger, and speaking in a loud voice, as if he were addressing a deaf person or a foreigner.

The old man pulled out a shilling and held it up.

'Saved it up,' said he, his voice whistling over his tooth. 'They give it me back all fair and square when I come out of the or-spidal.'

His neighbours fell back a little further. The old man took of his hat, and passing his hand over his head, said:

'Didn't substract nothing for shaving me neither.'

Some laughed: others, with more comprehensive faculties, shuddered.

Remarking the interest he had created, the old man continued:

'Been in the orspidal five weeks.' He pulled out his bottle of rum and held it up. 'That's what's been the matter with me. Dead hares been hunting me up and down, and dead childen, too.' He put away the bottle carefully, adding, as if to himself, 'Yes, dead childen and a dead wife, too.' He turned again to the people and, addressing them collectively with a wave of his horny hand, said, 'Don't you drink—none of you. It ain't good. It's bad. And when you once begin, you can't leave off. It makes you forget one hour, but it makes you remember twice as much the follerin' twenty-three. And the end of it is you must go to the orspidal because of the dead hares that chases you up and down. I'm going to cure myself, I am. Going to spend my shilling seein' sights instead of drinkin' rum. Dead hares as big as that!' he stretched his rum bottle out on one side and his shilling on the other, making a hideous grimace as he spoke; then his voice fell as he replaced the bottle in his pocket; 'and little childen, too—all dead.'

'Turn it up, master,' remonstrated the man nearest him. 'We've come here to enj'y ourselves.

'So we are,' answered the old man, with another attempt at a laugh. 'Come here to have a reg'lar good time, ain't we? To see things 'll make us laugh and forget, not things as makes you remember and cry, eh? They don't show you dead things in there, do they?' he asked doubtfully. 'No hares—no dear little dead babies?'

'I wish I hadn't come to-night anyway. It would give a chap the sick of play-going to hear you.'

The old man was gauging the width of the door with his eye now—speculating whether a dead hare of the size he was familiar with could follow him in. His tongue loosened, and he spoke out his thoughts.

'A nice thing if he's goin' to carry on like this all the evening!' muttered the younger man.

At this moment the door was unfastened, and in the press of the crowd the old fellow was carried, and pushed, and hustled down into the front row of the gallery. He was very satisfied with his position, and looked over the iron rail in front down into the pit with a chuckle. Then he looked round at the doors opening upon the gallery behind. From these his eyes turned with a scared look over the assembled audience, and then over the rails down into the pit. He noticed a gas-branch projecting from the boxes below, and nodded his head cheerfully—it was a good yard to the right of him.

By a cruel mischance the man who objected to his tone of conversation had unconsciously taken a seat next but one to him—an accident which he did not perceive until it was too late to get another seat, except in the back row. For some time he evaded the recognition of the old man, but at length he was alarmed by a tap on the arm—the old man, reaching before the intermediate spectator, attracted his attention.

With a grin and a nod of recognition, the old man said:

'Shall I tell you what I'll do if a dead hare comes in through one of those doors?— I shall jump over, down there. I shan't want to go to a orspidal to be cured then, shall I?'

The aggrieved man called a policeman, and complained of being annoyed.

'You must hold your row, or leave the house,' said the policeman to the old man, having heard the complaint against him.

'All right, policeman; I'll be quiet,' said the old man; adding, in a conciliatory tone to his offended neighbour, 'I'll shut my eyes, then I can't see any dead hares or poor little babies, eh?'

He took off his hat, and put it under the seat : then, making a pillow of his arms, crossed on the ledge before him, he laid his miserable old head upon them and shut his eyes.

Happily for himself and those about him, he slept through the first piece, and did not wake up until the burlesque had begun. The spectacle bewildered him for a while, but he grew accustomed to the strangeness of it. When the audience clapped, he clapped also, and was behind none when Folly came upon the stage. A change in his manner appeared directly he heard her voice; he became excited, and followed her with his eyes, trying to get a clear glimpse of her face.

'Make that old fellow sit down,' cried someone at the back.

He sat down without a word, still following Folly with his eyes. His neighbour saw him clutching the iron rails in front with quivering fingers. When the old man took his eyes from Folly, he turned them hurriedly behind him, and then down in the pit.

'Put your hand on the old man's jacket;

he's going to pitch himself over,' whispered the man who could not remove his observation.

Folly came down to the front singing. The old man heard her voice and saw her face fairly.

He sprang to his feet again.

'Sit down, you old fool!' said the man next to him, gripping his arm tightly.

'One word!' whispered the old man. 'Is she dead or not?'

'Dead? Of course not. That's Folly. If you go round to the stage-door you can see that she's alive for yourself.'

In a few minutes the gallery was freed from its unwelcome visitor. As quickly as he could leave the theatre the old man left it, and those who assisted his entrance showed an equal desire not to retard his exit.

*　*　*　*　*

When Folly left the theatre she was detained a moment under the gaslight at the stage-door by the doorkeeper addressing a whispered word to Roland Aveling, on whose arm her hand rested.

'There's an old man been hanging about the doors these two hours waiting to see Miss Folly—he seems a little off his head. I thought I'd put you on your guard,' said the doorkeeper.

'What is the matter?' asked Folly.

'Nothing much—a madman asking after you. Another you have frenzied with your eyes,' answered Roland.

'Where is he?'

'I don't know, miss; the police have driven him away.'

Folly, standing under the gas, lifted her veil, and looked up and down the street. Except the ordinary loiterers by the stage-door there was no one noticeable.

'He has gone,' said Roland. 'Come, you mustn't stand uncovered here for all the madmen in London.'

He led Folly down to the brougham: an attendant opened the door. Folly entered, and Roland prepared to follow as soon as she had arranged her skirts.

At that instant the door on the opposite side of the brougham opened. The uncovered and ghastly head of the old man was thrust in, and he caught hold of Folly's hand. She screamed in terror, looking upon the hideous face and head so close to hers, and tried to free her hand from his grasp.

'No, no!' cried the old man. 'She is not

dead—her hand lives! her voice lives! She is here, living and breathing, not dead and cold!' He set one foot in the brougham to enter. Folly screamed again, shrinking from the repulsive creature to the farther side of the carriage. Seeing the vacant place at her side, the old man prepared to take it, but before he could raise his second foot from the road, Roland, who had run round the carriage, seized him by the collar and dragged him out into the mud of the street.

A couple of policemen ran up and took the wet and muddy object from Roland's hands.

'Folly, Folly!' cried the old man, 'do not let them take me away to prison. Save me, save me! I am your father!'

CHAPTER IV.

A RECOGNITION.

THE policemen had the old man fast. He couldn't disengage his weak arms from the grasp of the powerful men, but his voice was still free.

'Save me, save me!' he cried; 'do not let them take me away. I am your father—John Morrison.'

Roland had returned to the carriage, and telling the driver to go on quickly, he put his foot into the brougham as it moved.

'Stop!' cried Folly, rising and knocking at the glass behind the driver. 'If that old man is my father he must not be left here,' she added, speaking in a voice of unwonted emotion to Roland.

'He will not be ill-treated. The police will liberate him when we are gone. It is some poor demented creature; he cannot be your father.'

'Why not?' answered Folly, angrily. 'Stop, I say! He shall not be left lying in the road at the mercy of those men— stop!'

The coachman pulled up, hearing the repeated command.

People were running past the brougham to join the crowd about the little group opposite the stage-door.

Folly turned the handle and threw the door open.

'For heaven's sake stay where you are, Folly! Let the driver go on. I will return and see that no harm comes to the old man,' said Roland, restraining the girl.

'You!' the girl answered, with passionate vehemence, trying to release her arm. 'You! is he *your* father?'

'Be calm; I will see that everything is right. It is not safe for you to go there in that crowd.'

'Do you think because I am a girl I am a coward? Let me go this instant. I hate you!'

She sprang out of the brougham, and Roland after her.

Her mother's spirit lived in Folly, and with her energy and strength she pushed through the idle crowd into the ring about the policemen and their captive.

'There, there, she has come to me! I said she would—my own daughter!' exclaimed John Morrison. 'My own beautiful daughter! You won't let me go to prison, will you? She is alive, not dead, like the little children. She doesn't hunt me up and down, but comes to save me—don't you, dear?'

'*Are* you my father?' asked Folly, recoiling instinctively as she looked at the repulsive figure before her, and half hiding her eyes behind her gloved hand.

'Yes, yes; you have Joan's skin and hair and mouth—all as I remember her when I coorted her long, long ago. And see there, by the side of your white glove, the very mole at the corner of the eye that she had. All just the same, and your hair, and your voice; it's like as if I looked at your mother in her pretty young days.'

'He's been drinking,' said the policeman, winking. 'Here, what's this you've got in your pocket, old 'un?—physic I'll be bound.'

'It's rum; but you shall have it if you'll only let me go, policeman. I haven't drunk a drop since tea-time—I haven't, I swear,' John Morrison turned to his daughter, 'and I won't. I'll be good, and do just what the doctors told me; only don't let them take me away.'

Folly, trembling, stood unable to speak.

'What shall we do with him?' asked the policeman, in a low voice of Roland. 'We can just pretend to take him to the station, and then let him off round the corner. Kind of frighten him, you know.'

Folly's irresolution passed away as her quick ear caught the suggestion.

'Let him go,' said she, firmly. 'This is my business, and only mine. Let him go this minute; I will take care of him.'

The constable looked doubtfully at Roland, and receiving no sign from him, relaxed his hold with a few words and a nod to his companion. John Morrison, finding himself free, ran to Folly's side, and clutching her arm with both hands, said:

'Quick—quick, dear, let us go away quick! Come—come, never mind my rum!'

Folly did not attempt to take her arm away. She looked into the grinning, hideous face so near her, and pointed to the brougham. He dragged her quickly towards it. Looking round to see if the policemen were following, he caught sight of Roland walking close to him.

'Who is that man? What does he want, dear daughter? See—the man who threw me into the road and set the policemen on to me. Take care of me, my dear. Don't let him throw me down again.'

By a rapid movement he changed his position and ran to the other side of Folly, taking that arm between his two hands and looking across her with a half-mad look at Roland.

When they came to the brougham he wrenched open the door and sprang in, impelled by the overpowering fear of being taken away and the hope of self-preservation. He dragged Folly in with desperate eagerness, and reaching over her, pulled the door to, holding the inner handle with both hands, and keeping his eyes on Roland with the terrified yet vicious look of a chimpanzee that has secured some coveted object.

Roland took the box-seat beside the driver.

'Will you let him come?' said John Morrison to Folly. 'Let me open the front window softly and push him over under the wheels.'

'No, no; he is kind and good. He will do you no harm!' answered Folly, speaking for the first time since she had liberated him.

'Kind and good—ha, ha!—to throw your father on the road! Never mind; I don't want to offend you, dear. You are not angry with me?'

'Oh no.'

'I'm glad he couldn't come inside with us. He can't come in, can he? There isn't room, is there? Spread out your dress, dear, so that he shan't think there is space for him to come between us. You won't let him separate us, will you? I don't like him at all; he looks like the man who set the dead hares to hunt me. Who knows but what he might turn into a dead hare himself, and hunt me up and down, up and down, up and down. I couldn't escape here. It isn't like being close to the rails of the theatre gallery, is it? One could escape there.'

'What do you mean?'

'I've been hunted, Folly dear—hunted by dead hares, sometimes as big as horses, sometimes larger than a haystack—hunted everywhere; and sometimes I have been followed by little dead children—your brothers and sisters, dear—all dead; and your mother, too, dear, poor thing!—dead. They hunted me out of my mind once, and I had to go to the orspidal, but they let me out, and took the dead things away. But if I saw 'em again I would jump somewheres as they couldn't follow me to: that's why I liked the front of the gallery. If they had followed me in there I could have jumped over and escaped, couldn't I? When I first saw you I thought you was dead; but you're not, are you, dear?'

'No, no, no; feel my hand.'

'Oh, you dear, kind daughter! Warm, isn't it?—quite alive; not cold and damp and green like the others. You wouldn't let a dead hare come near me, would you?'

'No, no; don't talk of that.'

'No, I won't talk of it,' answered the old man, putting his horny hand over his mouth and shaking his head. Presently his thoughts wandered away from the purpose of self-restraint, his hand slipped away, and he said, 'The dead hare did it, though. If it hadn't been for the dead hare I shouldn't have left my little ones and my wife to go in the work-house and die. All dead, all except you; you are alive, aren't you?'

Folly nodded and put her hand upon his. He smiled and giggled childishly, then he asked, with sudden eagerness:
'How old are you, Folly?'
'I am seventeen at Christmas-time.'
'That is the time; oh yes, you are my daughter!' Once more he cackled, rubbing his hands together gleefully. 'Just as I reckoned it. Every year I have said, now the little one is fifteen, now she is sixteen— like that. But I didn't know whether you were a girl or a boy. It was the hare did that. And your brothers and sisters and your mother? oh, what a lot I want to know! Come, let us begin quite at the beginning. We won't think about that thing that hunted me.' He shut his eyes and put his fingers in his ears until vague forgetfulness stole over him. Opening his eyes slowly, and looking at Folly with a sly, imbecile grin, he said, 'I've given it the slip. But why did they call you Folly? you were to be named Florence.'
'That was my name; but the people at the workhouse called me Folly for short.'
'What workhouse?'
'Chertsey—where I was born.'
'So they took my poor Joan thither.

Poor Joan—poor Joan!' He looked at the girl, and, as if afraid to speak, opened his mouth, forming the word 'dead?' and then put his hand over his lips. Folly understood the question.

'She died the same day I was born—Christmas Day.'

'That was the hare,' he said, nodding significantly. 'You never saw your brothers and sisters?'

'No.'

'All dead! all dead! We shall never find them, dear. They told me she went out to find me the night I was sent to prison for taking up that dead hare—no, it isn't drink, that is quite true—and she must have fallen by the way and been carried to Chertsey. Poor Joan—my poor Joan! What are you going to do with me?'

'Take you home with me.'

'Ha, ha, ha! what fun! Look here, we'll have this between us.' He felt in his pocket for the bottle. 'Ha, they took it away from me; but we will have a little drop of rum. Not much, just a little. That won't harm me, and I shall not be afraid of—that thing if I am in the same house with you. Just a little drop of rum, Folly dear. You will

A Recognition.   47

lend me threepence, won't you?—your old father.'

Folly nodded. The girl's tongue was tied. Her courage sank in the presence of this awful responsibility which had come to her.

Roland turned round to look through the front window and assure himself of Folly's safety. The light from the carriage lamp fell full upon his face. John Morrison shrunk into the corner, covering the lower part of his face with his hands and looking over his fingers.

Folly nodded to Roland.

'What are you making signs to him for?' whispered the old man, with quick suspicion.

'To let him know that I am quite safe.'

'You are not safe,' answered he, fumbling quickly in his trousers pocket.

Folly's flesh crept as he pulled out a big horn-handled knife, and unclasped a hook in the back of it which was intended to clean horse's hoofs.

'What are you going to do with that?' she asked.

'Don't be frightened, dear. You don't think I would hurt you, do you? I am going to protect you. The blade's broke, but this hook is better than nothing.'

'Put it away; there is nothing to fear.'

'Yes, there is. I don't like his look. He's just like the man that killed my Joan and my children, and sent me to prison, and made me the poor old wretch I am—only he's younger. Yes, younger. What is his name?'

'He is no one you know. He is good and kind.'

'What is his name?'

'Aveling.'

John Morrison gave a sharp cry that made Roland turn round again, bringing his face into the light once more.

The old man's bravery forsook him in an instant. He dropped the knife and cowered in a corner, holding his face in his hands as before.

'It's him, it's him!' he whispered hoarsely. 'I knew his fair face and blue eyes; but he's grown younger instead of older, like me. No one has hunted him.'

He felt at his feet stealthily for his knife, which he picked up as Roland removed his face from the glass.

'He isn't looking now. Let me break through the glass and tear him with this; I could, for your sake.'

'You shall do nothing of the kind; give me the knife,' said Folly, sternly.

A Recognition.

From maniacal fierceness John Morrison's expression changed to idiotic weakness. Sliding the instrument behind him, he said, in a tone of supplication:

'Let me keep it, Folly dear. I won't hurt him. But let me keep it in case he should hunt me away. He might turn into a hare, as he has done before, and hunt me up and down, up and down; and how could I escape without this?'

'Give it to me.'

He yielded it up, and she threw it out of the window.

'Now we are at his mercy,' said he, clasping his hands.

'We have nothing to fear.'

'You don't know him—I didn't know him —nobody knew him. Everybody thought him kind and good. But I tell you he killed your mother and her brood, and ruined me; does not that make you dread him? You are not dead, you say?'

'You are mistaken; he was a child when my mother died.'

'No, no, I'm not mistaken. I know his eyes and his face. You say his name is Aveling; but I should have known him without that. Hasn't he been hunting me ever since I was young and good-looking and happy, him and his keeper and the dead hare? Don't tell me I am mistaken: he is Sir Andrew.'

'Sir Andrew?'

'Sir Andrew Aveling grown young again, but him, with his wicked heart and kind face still.'

Folly was perplexed like an awakening sleeper between the real and the illusory. Facts came to prove that real which she had regarded as imaginary. She could no longer doubt that the old man beside her was her father; she could no longer disbelieve that the young man who had been kind to her was in some manner connected with the misery of her father. Roland had often spoken to her of his father, Sir Andrew; and she herself had detected a likeness between him and the little miniature of the baronet which he carried in a locket of his mother's upon his chain.

But a fresh anxiety arose to distract her. They were in Lambeth Road, and nearing her home the carriage slackened its pace. Before it came to a stand Roland leapt from the box. Simultaneously John Morrison, with no thought but for his own safety, burst open the door on the opposite side and sprang into the road.

'Go away, go away!' said Folly impatiently to Roland. 'You frighten him. Go away!'

'But I cannot leave you alone with him, Folly; he is dangerous.'

'He is my father, that is all I know. He has run away, and will not return while you are here. Leave me.'

'But——'

'Will you go away?' cried Folly, stamping her foot in angry impatience. 'It seems that I have more to fear from you than from him.'

Roland bowed and offered his hand. Folly turned her back on him without a word. Her father's words had taken deep effect upon her highly-wrought feelings, and she felt a repugnance to her admirer which she was too honest to conceal.

Roland withdrew discomfited. But he had no intention of relinquishing Folly to the fate of her own selection. Walking from the light, he perceived John Morrison on the opposite side of the way cowering by a buttress of the wall. Keeping his eyes that way and walking a few steps farther, he saw the old man dart from his hiding-place across the road, run up the steps to Folly standing at her door, and the next moment he heard the door shut with a loud noise.

He lingered in the neighbourhood, taking care to keep out of sight until the door opened and Miss Clip came out with a bottle.

'She is quite safe; the old man is like a baby in her hands,' said she, in answer to Roland's eager questioning. 'He is only afraid of you. I am going to fetch a quartern of rum for them. It will be all right, sir, don't fear.'

Despite this assurance, Roland walked about in the vicinity of the house for a long while after the last light had disappeared from its windows, and left it with a fervent prayer for the safety and happiness of the young actress.

Friendship is generous and disinterested, but could any man, not in love with the girl, forget that she had sent out for rum to drink with her mad father?

CHAPTER V.

THE FILIAL LOVE OF FOLLY.

THE natural spring of affection in Folly's heart, which had been pent up for so many years, burst forth with accumulated force and added volume, now that a course was opened for its flow. Filial love attained its highest development in her emotional young breast. Attachments of a more or less transient kind she had formed for several individuals since her coming to London; but they were for the most part mere expressions of gratitude. Not one of them was tinged with passion, or arose from that feeling of unselfish love which comes spontaneously from the heart and owes nothing to reciprocal considerations.

'He is my father!' Folly needed no other

argument for loving John Morrison than that. His terrible condition, his hideous appearance, which made him repulsive to others, which at first shocked her beauty-loving senses, served only to endear him more strongly to her when she found that he was her father, by appealing to her compassion and exciting her womanly pity.

Women admire the strong, but they love the weak. To comfort the unhappy, to minister to the wants of the helpless, satisfies the instinctive craving to be of use in this world, which animates every heart not utterly depraved, and is in woman least disguised.

Folly felt for her father as a mother feels for her deformed child-babe, loving him the more because he was loved by none but her. The time that she had devoted to her own pleasures she devoted to pleasing him. She dressed him like a gentleman, gave him luxuries that she denied herself, bought him presents and flowers and books with pictures, which she taxed her imagination to explain to his weak understanding. Learning from a physician that her father's dementia was due to excessive drinking, and that the next attack of delirium would probably be fatal, she used all her efforts to wean him from his vice, stimulating his appetite for healthier substitutes, wheedling him, coaxing him, cheating him out of his darling pleasure. Pretending to share the glass with him, she more than half intoxicated herself with rum —a spirit most vile and detestable to her palate, in order to lessen his portion.

Hers was an arduous undertaking, for the old man had no conscience now : he lied and stole to satisfy his cravings. She gave him everything but money ; but he, with the cunning of a drunkard and a lunatic, contrived to get money to buy rum. He crept out in her absence and pawned the things she had given him—books, pictures, dress, anything that could be converted into money; and this despite his fear of meeting Sir Andrew Aveling and being carried away to prison, or hunted by dead hares.

Folly could not induce him to go with her for walks in the day-time. Fears for himself were not to be overcome by love for her—by nothing but his passion for rum.

The love was, as in many cases, alas ! all on one side.

He was as selfish as a child, and loved her just for what he could get. He would have bartered her away body and soul for a bottle of rum; he would have sold himself for the same price. The more difficult he found it to obtain what he wanted, the greater pleasure he had in getting it. It was a mad lust, that made him perfectly oblivious of every consequence and of every consideration but the one idea of self-gratification.

And this man she loved with all the fulness of her nature.

Love has no eyes; but filial love might be represented without a head, for reason has no dominion over it.

When John Morrison talked, it was of himself and of the past. He told her of his young days, of his strength, his sober, steadfast life, of his early love for Joan—of her beauty, her virtues, her wifely love, her motherly tenderness; of his pride in keeping honest despite the hard times and temptations; of their hopes for the youngsters just going out to work; of their simple preparation for spending Christmas Day with the children, 'All together and comfortable like, wi' a pudden and a bit o' meat;' and then he explained the injustice done to him, his committal to prison, the break-up of his home, and the ruin of his family.

He scarcely mentioned Ledger's name,

always regarding him as the mere instrument of his master—a servant who did the dirty work he was paid to do. It was against Sir Andrew that he launched every angry invective that rose from his turbid imagination. He was the false witness, the unjust judge, the unrighteous justice, who with a stroke of the pen had consigned him to perdition, had murdered his wife, and scattered his helpless children, so that for him they were lost for ever; he who still pursued him, and would hunt him down to his death.

The border-line that divides madness from reason was obliterated from John Morrison's mind; he could not distinguish the real from the imaginary. The dead hare that hunted him, the dead wife and children who pursued him with their wan, supplicating faces, were to him as real as those substantial facts that dwelt in his memory.

Folly distinguished the two, but she did not allow for prejudice. She did not see that her father was unjust in attributing to Sir Andrew the crime committed by his servant, James Ledger. She believed implicitly in her father's view, and regarded Sir Andrew as alone responsible for all the misfortunes which had befallen her family.

He had, by an arbitrary and unjust use of the power vested in him, wrecked her father, killed her mother, and scattered her brothers and sisters to the mercy of the world. She knew that Roland had no part in the crime, and was guiltless of any sinister intentions against herself or her father—a knowledge which John Morrison could not and would not accept. He insisted that the man who had thrown him down in the street was 'Sir Andrew grown young.' Every day he questioned Folly about him.

'Where is he?—where is Sir Andrew?' he asked.

'He is in the country. At Aveling Hall. I have asked about him,' replied Folly.

'Who did you ask?'

'His son.'

'Don't you believe it, Folly dear--don't you believe it. He is Sir Andrew, deceiving you that you may deceive me. But I am not such a fool. I know the man who looked through the window at me. Do you think I could forget his blue eyes and fair face? Oh, what a fool I was not to dig my hook into his back as he sat there!'

'That man will do you no harm.'

'He told you so, and you believe him.

But you won't believe me, though I have suffered by him for your sake. He talks kindly to you that he may get you on his side to hunt me. And that is what you will do : you will help him to hunt me, and open my door to let in the dead hare. He watches outside the house ; he waits for the door to be opened. But you won't let him in, will you, dear Folly ? You won't take his part ? You won't let him take me away to the heath where he can hunt me, and there is nowhere for me to escape him ? Do tell me you won't, Folly dear.'

' I won't, father; you know I won't.'

' But you love him more than you do me. He has deceived you because you are a silly little fool, and he sees that you want to get rid of me.'

' No, father dear, no ; you are mistaken.'

' No, I am not. Why didn't you let me kill him, you wretch ? Why do you talk to him about me if you don't love him ?'

' I don't talk to him about you.'

' Don't you, Folly dear; don't you ? Not a word, eh ? Not a word ? Don't you tell him where I sleep ? Don't you tell him that I sometimes go out alone when you are at the theatre ?'

'Never. I do not say a word about you.'

'I would believe you if you were kinder to me—more good. Oh, how can you think of your poor mother and the little children—all dead, and look at me, no longer a handsome, honest, strong young man, but a toothless, ugly old thief, praying them not to hunt me from my grave, but to let me drop into it and be buried—how can you do this and love him, you heartless devil?'

'I don't love him. I love only you, father dear.' Folly clasped his arm to her breast.

'Do you? Do you love me well enough to tell *him* lies? Will you say I am dead and buried, that he may cease to hunt me—cease to set the great dead thing tracking me up and down wherever I go?'

'Yes, I will tell him that.'

'And will you send the girl out for a little rum, darling? Just a little to mix with a great deal of water, you know, and both drink out of the same glass, eh? Quite fair, you know; and you keep your hand on the glass so that I shan't drink more than my share. You always do drink fair, I know. You are so truthful and kind to me, dear. Never drink more than your share, or pour water in when you send me out of the room to look for some more—never. And there always is some more outside when you send me out for it ; only I can't find it because I'm such an old fool. Oh, no, dear, you never deceive me, you're so good. Just a little drop in a bottle, darling ; not the big bottle, dear. And the girl won't half fill the bottle with water while she's out! Oh no, she never does! You are all so truthful and so kind to the poor old man. Ha, ha, ha! Just a little drop—eh, dear?

It was in this way the argument usually finished ; for Folly would give way to the old man, cheating him, as he knew full well. Sometimes she refused obstinately, and then he would return to fierce reproaches, and work himself up into a terrible agony of suspicion and dread.

Under the influence of her father, Folly's character exhibited a marked change. On the stage she was the same, but off it she was no longer the thoughtless, careless, artless girl she had been.

An ignorant, impulsive girl, knowing no law but the *lex talionis* taught by the drama, and regarded as just and holy by all the less cultivated exponents of the drama—a law, unfortunately, which is taught from the pulpit as well as the stage—she heard of the cruel wrongs by which her family had suffered, and felt that to revenge them was a duty she owed to her miserable father and her dead mother. She came to look upon vengeance as a necessity, and upon herself as the natural minister. As her eyes rested upon her degraded father, she thirsted like a young savage to reduce Sir Andrew to the state of misery he had brought upon the old man. She was told that it was good to read the Bible, to believe in it as a Divine inspiration which could not err, to obey the laws it prescribed, and she learnt this verse by heart: 'And thine eye shall not pity; but life shall go for life, eye for eye, tooth for tooth, hand for hand, foot for foot.' Was she to blame for believing herself justified in executing the savage instinct of vengeance in her heart?

Not in a day, a week, or a month did she come to the determination to revenge the wrongs of her father; it crept upon her little by little, until it possessed her entirely.

Insidiously this wrong doctrine sapped the foundations of her generous and simple disposition—the bad taking the place of the good.

Long before she had formed any definite scheme for the destruction of Sir Andrew, she had assailed his son. Roland, she knew, was in her power.

CHAPTER VI.

A STRANGE VENGEANCE.

EARLY in the new year a ball was given by certain noblemen and gentlemen to selected members of the dramatic profession. Next to the titled names Roland Aveling, Esq., took the first place upon the committee list. None had subscribed more liberally than he.

About midnight the guests began to arrive. It was nearly one when the brougham brought Folly to the doors. Despite the hour, a considerable crowd had accumulated to see the public favourites pass. When Roland gave his hand to Folly, the spectators pressed forward to see her; as she stepped down upon the red cloth they greeted her with a sudden exclamation of admiration. She was recognised, and 'Folly!' 'Folly!' passed from lip to lip. Her ear was never dull to applause, and, hearing her name, she turned her head from side to side with a good-humoured smile and a nod. The public were her best friends, and she would acknowledge them at any time, no matter how she was dressed or in whose company she happened to be.

Conscious of her beauty and the effect she should make, she walked into the ball-room erect, and with the carriage of a princess. She was not mistaken as to her reception; the men hovered buzzing about her like bees, the women showed the disposition of wasps.

'Show me the lords,' said Folly to Roland.

'There is Lord Lancefoil on the right, looking at you. Shall I introduce you?'

'Oh no. He will introduce himself directly,' answered Folly, fixing her eyes on the nobleman. 'Show me some more.'

Roland pointed out the titled men, and Folly, having in turn magnetised each of them with those loadstones, her eyes, they gravitated towards her.

It was her first ball. Roland, in putting his name down upon her programme, instructed her in its use. She showed it to him after her first dance. It was filled up.

'All lords,' said she, 'except one.'

'Myself,' answered Roland, looking down the names. 'I wish I had a title, for your sake, Folly.'

'I like you just as well without. You are worth more to me than all the rest put together.'

Roland pressed the hand that rested on his arm to his side, and looked into the girl's face. She met his eyes, and subdued them with her bolder glance; then laughed lightly.

Lord Lancefoil came up, and claimed her hand as the music began. She pinched Roland's arm slyly, as she withdrew her hand. He did not dance, but stood watching her as she floated round the room, and she rewarded him with sweet smiles and languishing looks as she passed. When the waltz was over, she came to his side again.

'Why didn't you dance?' she asked.

'It was enough happiness to look at you,' he replied.

'Will you not dance except with me?'

'No.'

He took the programme from his vest pocket and tore it up.

'You are a good boy. I should have been ever so jealous if you had danced with anyone else.'

'Do you like this kind of dancing as well as you expected?'

'Yes. Waltzing is delicious. But I wish I might have you for a partner every time; no one dances as you do.'

The latter part of this speech was true in an equivocal sense. Roland was a clumsy dancer, but he had the happiness to be ignorant of the fact, and, taking Folly's words in their flattering sense, he pitied her for having to dance with less graceful dancers. Men are vainer than women, and more easily deceived.

He danced with Folly again, and took her to supper in high spirits. They were both excited, but Folly was careful about her wine. Roland, on the other hand, drank more than was good for him, and in the subsequent dance had a confused notion as to the position of the room and the relative distance of other dancers, with whom he would undoubtedly have come into collision but for his partner's guidance.

He contrived to get through the dance with no more serious accident than the tear-ing off about a couple of yards of the Honiton lace which covered Folly's blue satin dress, with one of the diamond sprays that had looped it up.

What did that matter?

'You shall have a new dress and more diamonds for the next ball,' he said, as he sat panting at Folly's side.

Not to cloy him with sweetness, Folly ceased to flatter him, and bestowed her smiles upon other partners in the succeeding dances. He watched her for a while with morose jealousy, and then went to the refreshment-room and drank more champagne. It excited without exhilarating him, and he returned to the ball-room in a humour to quarrel with anyone—Folly included. It took him some time to discover her among the waltzers, and then it was with difficulty he could follow her with his eyes. He was still straining his eyes to find her, when, taking the seat by his side, she put her hand on his arm, and said, with a laugh :

'For Heaven's sake don't look like that, Roland. Your eyes are nearly out of your head, and you are squinting most horribly.'

'I am sorry,' he said, turning to her with an air of offended dignity, which was ill-supported by the expression of his eyes and the articulation of his words; 'I am very sorry that I have ceased to give you pleasure.'

'You have not ceased. Don't you see how I am enjoying myself?'

'Yes; but I p'ceive your 'njoyment is perfec'ly in'ependent of any efforts on my part.'

'You stupid old fellow, you are jealous. You don't like me to be happy when you are not; and, indeed, I can't be, Roland,' said Folly, with sudden gravity.

A man's weaknesses cling to him in intoxication; the pliability of Roland's disposition, which led him at all times to yield to a gentle word, was evident in the readiness with which he responded to Folly's overture. With a sudden transition from dignity to sweetness he smiled at his companion, and said:

'Can't you be happy when I am not, Folly?'

'No. See, the waltz is not finished yet; I refused to dance another round when I saw how distressed you were.'

The new emotion sobered Roland.

'And you, who love dancing, did this for my sake? Oh, Folly, what a brute I am to let you see I was hurt, and what a fool to feel hurt. Didn't I bring you to enjoy yourself, and could I expect that you would make yourself ridiculous by sitting out? Oh, forgive me, *dear!*'

The word slipped out unconsciously. He had so guarded his tongue that the first term of endearment had never escaped him. He had bought her diamonds, and spent a small fortune on the ball-dress she wore, but always under the delusion that he was acting in simple friendship—a wilful delusion, which was maintained solely by that one slight restriction he put upon his lips. That was gone, and the result, even to his muddled senses, made him tremble to think of.

Folly caught the word, and, leaning towards him with melting eyes, whispered:

'What is there I could not forgive *you?*'

'You shall not suffer by my vile temper. Go, Folly, and finish this waltz.'

'Only with you.'

He jumped up, the blood rushing to his face and throbbing in his temples. How gloriously beautiful the girl was! If he lost everything and possessed only her, would he not be compensated?

As he put his arm about her, and clutched

her hand with passionate haste, the waltz ended.

'Never mind, we will dance the next dance together. What is it?'

She held out the programme she could not read.

'A galop. You are engaged for it to Lord Lancefoil.'

'What does that matter? What is he to me? I will dance with you.'

'He will be hurt.'

'What do I care who suffers, so that I give you happiness?'

Her eyes seemed to penetrate his very soul. He could not speak. He shivered, as if he were seized with cold; his tongue clove to the roof of his mouth.

'Tell me what you are thinking about,' said Folly, in a soft, low tone, dropping her soft gloved hand on his, as it rested on the cushion between them.

He turned his hand and caught her fingers, and was about to answer when Lord Lancefoil stepped in front of them.

This untimely interruption served to make his dismissal a work of pleasure to Folly. Very briefly she informed him that she had given the preference to Mr. Aveling as a partner for the next dance.

'It is easier to forgive Folly than her partner,' said the nobleman, with a bow, and withdrew, mentally cursing Folly, nevertheless.

And then the music commenced, and Roland rose at once, with a last struggle to preserve his tottering honour.

The galop is a dance which does not admit of much conversation during its performance, happily. Roland only replied to Folly's remarks, but his fingers spoke. Their linked hands formed a chain for the electric current of passion, and its fires shot from their eyes as they met and parted.

'I am thirsty,' said Folly, as the dance ended.

They went to the refreshment-room and drank champagne. They sat over their wine, and drank while others danced.

'There's Catesby looking for you; this is his dance,' said Roland.

'Let him go. I will dance with no one but you.'

'Folly!'

'Would you like me to?'

'No. Take your eyes away; they are too beautiful.'

'Drink to them, Roland.'

He filled the glasses to the brim.

'To your eyes, darling!' he cried fervidly, and drank the wine down to the last drop.

'You have not touched your glass, Folly.'

'How can I drink to my own eyes. Fill again, and I will give you a toast we may both drink.'

'Waiter, another bottle.'

The wire clicked, the cork popped, the wine frothed out into the glasses.

Roland took up his glass with a wavering hand.

'Your toast, Folly, your toast!'

She put her disengaged hand out and gave it to his eager grasp, and, leaning over the little table until her hair touched his cheek and her breath came warm upon his ear, she murmured:

'To Love!'

* * * * *

It was still dark, though the labourers were going to their work, when Folly took her seat in the brougham beside Roland, who had been lifted into the vehicle in a speechless and helpless state of intoxication. She was as self-composed and fresh as if she had undergone no excitement, and refused the assistance offered her by several friends of Roland, protesting that she was not afraid, and could take care of him.

As the carriage moved Roland slid towards her from the corner where he was propped up. She pushed him away with an expression of disgust, and, as she looked upon him in his besotted debasement, her thoughts were divided between him and her father.

She saw in Roland now something of her father's loathsomeness: but as she had wept over the shame of one, so she rejoiced in the vileness of the other. Retribution had begun. She prayed from her heart that Sir Andrew might suffer for his son as she suffered for her father.

Her purpose was unshaken by one compassionate thought. She had schooled herself to cruelty. 'And thine eye shall not pity; but life shall go for life, eye for eye, tooth for tooth, hand for hand, foot for foot.' These words she repeated again and again.

When the carriage stopped before Roland's chambers at Kensington, it was clear that help would be required to get the young man from the brougham.

The driver rang the bell. The housekeeper came to the door.

'Got Mr. Aveling in the kerridge,' said the driver, jerking his thumb over his shoulder.

'Mr. Aveling?'

'Yes, he's not quite well; took a little po'rly.' The driver spoke in a loud voice for Folly to hear, and winked significantly for the housekeeper to understand. 'The po'r gentleman can't walk comfor'ably. Have you got ere a man about that can help me carry him upstairs?'

'Why, there's a friend of his that came last night, and has occupied his room since. I'll go and fetch him.'

The housekeeper disappeared, and after a while returned with a tall, large-boned man, wrapped in one of Roland's gorgeous dressing-gowns.

The brougham door was opened, and Roland Aveling, in the contemptible position of a helpless drunkard by the side of a fresh and smiling girl, was displayed to the eyes of the Reverend Richard Vane.

CHAPTER VII.

A CHECK.

THE vicar of St. Barnabas, Tangley, looked neither disgusted nor surprised at the spectacle presented to his eyes. His expression was that of a strong man undergoing a necessary operation; the muscles of his brows and mouth were contracted as if with pain; that was all.

He took Roland's hand and shook it, trying to arouse him from his torpor. Roland gave no responsive sign of life. His hand dropped from the vicar's like a thing of lead. He was dead drunk.

'I must detain you while the coachman assists me in carrying my friend to his room,' he said, fixing his eyes upon Folly for the first time.

Folly inclined her head, not taking her eyes from Richard Vane's face.

They recognised each other by Roland's descriptions, and their eyes met with the measuring glance of foes.

It was thus the good and the bad angel met over the body of the man whose soul they were to fight for.

Folly tried to scan the capacities of the man who would thwart her purpose if he could; Richard Vane gauged the strength of the woman whose influence over Roland he was to counteract. Each read the other's thoughts.

'You are Mr. Vane?' said Folly.

'Yes; and you are Folly,' he replied.

She nodded with a little smile of defiance. The vicar turned to his friend, not without hope that a girl so young and beautiful might be directed into goodness.

He held the belief that loveliness and goodness are inseparable. There was nothing radically vicious in Folly's face to his eyes; its blemish was the result of wrong cultivation, which better training might remove.

He lifted his friend from the brougham.

He passed his hands under the helpless man's arms and clasped them on his breast, the coachman lifted his legs, and so together they carried Roland upstairs. In consideration of the care with which the coachman executed his part of the work Mr. Vane gave him a shilling and dismissed him with thanks; then, closing the door, he returned to the inner room, where Roland sat piled up in a big chair.

He shook up the bed he had been lying in, beat up the pillows, and turned back the sheets. Next he turned over the linen in the wardrobe until he found a clean nightshirt. After that he set to work on Roland himself. With a good deal of trouble he contrived to get him out of his evening and into his night dress. Then, tackling his patient as firemen serve suffocated persons, he got him upon his shoulder, and in that way carried him over to the bed, where he laid him down quietly, straightened him out, and covered him over with as much care and tenderness as if he had been the most gracious of sufferers. Having done this, the good Samaritan went into the next room, put out the light, and laid himself down on the couch to take his own proper share of rest.

aside, and marked another drop flow down the damp surface and drop off upon the sheet as the young man drank. Then the Samaritan's heart rejoiced, and his eye grew moist in sympathy.

'Now turn your back to the light and have another doze. You'll be able to get up when you wake again,' said he, when Roland, lowering his head, held out the empty glass.

Roland turned his back without a word, and drew the clothes over his head.

The vicar looked on, standing beside the bed with the glass in his hand and silently puffing at his pipe. The shoulders beneath the clothes were agitated with a quick convulsive movement. The vicar, sitting on the edge of the bed, bent over and patted his friend soothingly.

Roland threw back the clothes, caught hold of the vicar's hand and kissed it.

It was a hand to kiss, being unsoiled as God had fashioned it. Never had it been used in any mean or unworthy work; never had it been withdrawn when humanity demanded its help.

*   *   *   *

After a couple of hours' sleep Roland

awoke considerably refreshed. A cold bath completely restored him to his habitual vigour. He came from his bedroom with a blush for his past weakness, but with less fear than he had anticipated, and sat down with Vane to the tea and steak prepared for him.

Richard Vane also ate.

'Have some more steak,' he said, dividing the portion and helping himself; 'you will get nothing more to eat until supper-time.'

Roland looked up inquiringly.

'How's that?' he asked.

'You are going to Tangley with me, and I leave Waterloo by the 5.30.'

'I don't see how I can do that.'

'Why?'

'In the first place,' said Roland, after a little consideration, 'in the first place, there's my father.'

'Is he in the first place?' asked Vane, looking up sharply. 'Come, Roland, start fair.'

'I admit I didn't think of him first. But I have an engagement—that is, I am expected at the Levity to-night.'

'We shall pass a telegraph office on our way to the station, or you can get a messenger to aside, and marked another drop flow down the damp surface and drop off upon the sheet as the young man drank. Then the Samaritan's heart rejoiced, and his eye grew moist in sympathy.

'Now turn your back to the light and have another doze. You'll be able to get up when you wake again,' said he, when Roland, lowering his head, held out the empty glass.

Roland turned his back without a word, and drew the clothes over his head.

The vicar looked on, standing beside the bed with the glass in his hand and silently puffing at his pipe. The shoulders beneath the clothes were agitated with a quick convulsive movement. The vicar, sitting on the edge of the bed, bent over and patted his friend soothingly.

Roland threw back the clothes, caught hold of the vicar's hand and kissed it.

It was a hand to kiss, being unsoiled as God had fashioned it. Never had it been used in any mean or unworthy work; never had it been withdrawn when humanity demanded its help.

* * * *

After a couple of hours' sleep Roland

awoke considerably refreshed. A cold bath completely restored him to his habitual vigour. He came from his bedroom with a blush for his past weakness, but with less fear than he had anticipated, and sat down with Vane to the tea and steak prepared for him.

Richard Vane also ate.

'Have some more steak,' he said, dividing the portion and helping himself; 'you will get nothing more to eat until supper-time.'

Roland looked up inquiringly.

'How's that?' he asked.

'You are going to Tangley with me, and I leave Waterloo by the 5.30.'

'I don't see how I can do that.'

'Why?'

'In the first place,' said Roland, after a little consideration, 'in the first place, there's my father.'

'Is he in the first place?' asked Vane, looking up sharply. 'Come, Roland, start fair.'

'I admit I didn't think of him first. But I have an engagement—that is, I am expected at the Levity to-night.'

'We shall pass a telegraph office on our way to the station, or you can get a messenger to carry a letter. I think I know who expects you. If everything else fails, I will stay in London and carry your excuses myself.'

'That is not necessary,' Roland replied, staring at the table, on which he was industriously scraping the crumbs together with his knife.

'Then, now for your second objection.'

'My father—you know the terms of my agreement with him?'

'Yes; and like them none the better for knowing them well. That agreement must be broken.'

'If I break it I destroy the hope of giving Madge a position.'

'What kind of position do you think you are likely to give her by keeping it?' asked the vicar, drily. Roland winced.

'You will remember,' continued Vane, 'that besides your agreement with your father you have one with my sister. It must be clear to anyone who does not wilfully deceive himself that both contracts cannot be kept; and the question I ask you to decide at once is which of these do you feel most binding upon you?'

'You can answer that for yourself, Dick.'

'I have answered it. I answered it to my

own satisfaction, and it should be to yours, when I said you would go to Tangley to night.'

'It depends upon the justice of your assertion that I cannot keep both contracts.'

'That requires no argument. I have seen sufficient of Folly to know that she is dangerous.'

'How do you think she can hurt me?'

'I am not thinking of you, Roland; I was thinking of Madge.'

Roland was silenced by this home-thrust.

'These interesting experiments you are making on yourself jeopardise her happiness. Breaking your contract and breaking her heart might be the same thing.'

'How can you think I would do either?'

'You have gone as far towards doing so as you could. You deluded yourself with the idea that you were strong enough to resist temptation; you persuaded Madge to share that delusion. You are not keeping your contract when you depart from the character you professed to have and promised to maintain when you made it.'

'You mustn't damn a good horse for a stumble, Dick.'

'Good horse, indeed! Don't flatter yourself. Stumble, forsooth! You only keep on your legs by accident. Do you think I came here last night on the off-chance, to choose your own horsey language, of catching you stumbling? The only off-chance I looked for was of finding you at home with a pipe and one of your silly yellow hermaphrodite novels. It is no secret that you have been dangling about in the *coulisses* every night for the last two months. A good horse, indeed!' the vicar laughed contemptuously; 'why, you've nothing of the mule but his obstinacy, and the jackass would cease to bray if he had not more resolution than you.'

'How you work a fellow's words against him if he happen to make a simile! You're precious hard on a man. I thought you were going to take some compassion on a poor devil of a fellow.'

'So I would if you would not persist in declaring that you're *not* a poor devil. I know you're a poor devil, and I pity you. All the world must pity such a poor devil.'

'There you go again, Dick; "poor devil, poor devil," half-a-dozen times in a minute.'

'If you are satisfied that you are a pitiable object, that is enough. It is not a novelty to me to regard you in that light.

The knowledge that you had not enough strength to keep you out of mischief, to keep you from hurting yourself and others as well, brought me here. As you wouldn't fly from temptation, it was necessary for some one to come and carry you, poor thing.'

'I can't understand you—one moment kind, the next harsh.'

'I hope I may be blind and deaf the day a sufferer leaves me without a lessened woe; but I hope I may lose all my senses before I encourage professional beggars.'

'Who's a professional beggar?'

'Who is a professional beggar? Why, he who gets compassion that he does not deserve; he who begs others to help him because he is too lazy to help himself; he who sorts over the crusts you give him, taking those which are palatable and wasting the rest; he who deserves rather a horsewhip than a kind word; he who takes but never gives; he who prays for himself and never thinks of others.'

The vicar ceased to speak, and Roland buried his face in his hands. Presently the young fellow lifted his head.

'Oh, Madge, how have I forgotten you!' he cried, springing to his feet, forgetful of

Richard, and thinking only of his sister. 'And when I have told you all, how can you forgive me?'

'If you tell her all,' said the vicar, in his sweetest tones, coming to Roland's side and laying his hand affectionately on his shoulder, 'she will trust you and forgive you as only a woman can.'

CHAPTER VIII.

ROLAND SAYS 'NO.'

ROLAND'S obstinacy being overcome, he was eager to pursue the new course open to him, which had to his impulsive nature the additional charm of newness. Imagination painted the future in pleasant colours, and took no notice of unsightly obstructions. He was incapable of looking fairly over anything: his eye would only rest on those objects which harmonised with the mood of his mind.

At Waterloo the vicar led him to the telegraph office.

'You forget that someone expects you to-night,' Vane explained, in answer to Roland's look of inquiry.

He felt almost ashamed to write the telegram. 'I shall be unable to see you to-night; I will write to you soon,' were the words he sent to Folly—words sufficiently significant of his intention to see her no more.

They took possession of the corners of a smoking compartment and buried themselves in their newspapers — the vicar to give Roland opportunity for thought, and he to avail himself of the opportunity.

What should he say to Margaret? Of course he should let her know that he was determined to marry her at once; but then how could he explain this sudden and unannounced determination? Must he tell her all? Would it not pain her to learn how he had got drunk, and all that? Was it not one of those 'rude experiences unmeet for ladies' even to hear of? Would it not be kinder to refer in the slightest manner possible to Folly? She would have to learn something, but how much? Richard Vane had declared that his dangling about in the *coulisses* was no secret. Who had told him?

'Dick, who told you that I sometimes went behind the scenes at the Levity?' he asked.

'Who told me that you went six nights in the week behind the scenes at the Levity?' responded the vicar, with a smile. 'An old friend of yours.'

'Amadis Garnier, I'll go odds.'

'You've won. Book it. Amadis Garnier it was.'

'I don't think that was exactly consistent with his professions of friendship, do you?'

'Yes. If he hadn't had a good opinion of you he would have thought you wished to conceal the fact.'

'That's very cleverly turned, Dick; but it doesn't exactly fit the case. I mean that it is hardly consistent with professed friendship to interfere with another man's personal affairs. He came preaching a sermon to me on the subject about a week after I had made the acquaintance of Folly, and when he couldn't possibly have any reason to think I was in danger.'

'That is why he preached his sermon, I dare say,' replied the vicar, taking up his paper again.

'You shan't read, Dick, though you are venomous. When did this precious fellow that calls himself my friend tell you about me?'

'About a month ago. He stayed with us through Christmas, and returned to London with me yesterday. We had a very pleasant Christmas Day, though it will displease you, perhaps, to hear that the man who calls himself your friend proposed your health when we were all sitting round the fire after supper.'

'Did he though? Well, that was thoughtful and kind—just like him. I mean that he's—a jolly good fellow with all his faults. Did Madge drink to me?'

'Yes; she dropped a diamond from her eye into the glass and drank it to you.'

'Oh, Dick!'

'And I thought of you when I was reading divine service.'

'Did you, Dick?'

'I prayed for your enemies, persecutors, and slanderers—Amadis Garnier included—and that their hearts might be turned.'

'Scoffer.'

Roland did not refer to the subject again until they were nearing the vicarage.

'Does Madge know that you went to town to fetch me?' he asked

'No.'

'Did Garnier blurt out before her that I—about the Levity?'

'No. You will have to tell Madge all that she should know.'

Roland felt relieved. He had already decided that all Madge should know was just as much as it would be agreeable for her to hear and for him to tell.

The evening was damp and misty and mild; the ground yielded beneath the foot. An old woman carrying a large umbrella was the only person they met between the station and the vicarage. The clock of St. Barnabas struck seven. Roland thought of the Strand thronged with people, cheerful with many lights, where one might travel rapidly in a hansom with comfort in the worst weather. Never had the country seemed so dull, dreary, and unpleasant as now. He thought of the theatre, where not a moment was without its excitement, and then of Folly, with her lovely little face and sparkling gaiety. Would she miss him, poor little soul? Would she think him heartless —and for the first time be sad? Would she read all in that brief telegram that it implied, and be heartbroken by his sudden desertion? Would she think him mean and treacherous, or would her tender heart forgive him? Would she shed a tear, or—horrible thought!—would she laugh, as if nothing had happened, and flirt with another man in his absence? A feeling of sickness came with the jealous suspicion. He looked about him—his eyes could not penetrate the mist beyond the sober vicar walking along by his side. All the uses of the world he was to live in seemed weary, stale, flat, and unprofitable. His palate craved for a glass of brisk champagne—one glass would do him all the good in the world, giving vitality to his sluggish spirit, and encouraging him to do his duty. He would get nothing but beer at the vicarage, and the thought of that simple beverage made him shudder. He felt that it would make his liver worse instead of better.

'Beastly hole!' he said to himself, as they came into the village, where a candle burning dimly on the counter of the general shop was the only light to be seen. And this was where he must live and find contentment. Should he never see Folly again? What on earth would he find to do all day?

After the dissipation of the preceding night he would have been miserable anywhere; but here the distemper attained to its utmost malignancy in the absence of that excitement which appeared to be its sole remedy.

He found some relief on arriving at the vicarage. Lights shone with a warm glow through the rose curtains of the latticed door, and his mind was occupied in conjecturing how Madge would look when she saw him.

She herself opened the door to her brother's knock, and catching sight of Roland in the background, was joyfully surprised. She held his hand between hers, and said, in a voice of tender love :

'I am so glad you have come.'

If Richard Vane had not assured him to the contrary, Roland would have imagined she expected his coming.

'That's the worst of having a character for impulsiveness,' he replied, laughing ; 'you can never surprise anyone.'

Madge would rather he had been silent, for his words were utterly dissonant with her sentiments. It was not impulse that had led her to pray for his coming, nor did she pray that impulse might bring him to her—quite otherwise.

Roland's contrition was nothing but an impulse ; he had spoken truly in jest. He felt no sincere delight in returning to Margaret, no genuine satisfaction in having escaped temptation. He knew that he ought to love Margaret ten times more than Folly, but the consciousness that he did not made it more impossible that he should. Moreover, the honesty at the bottom of this young man's heart revolted at the hypocrisy he felt it necessary to practise. Had he only had the courage to be true to himself, all would have gone well.

Conscious of his own deficiencies, he attempted to appear natural by assuming an air of gaiety which was as unpleasant to Margaret and Richard as if he had openly professed his careless indifference to their happiness. They could not respond to his lively sallies, and their irresponsiveness impressed him more deeply with the idea that the country was awfully dull, and that in leaving London he had made a great sacrifice for the sake of duty.

After supper Richard retired to his study with a significant nod to Roland. Margaret folded her hands on her knee and bent her head, turning a little pale as her brother closed the door behind him.

'How the deuce shall I begin? Hang it! he might have given me till to-morrow!'

thought Roland. However, there was no avoiding the difficulty, so he crossed the room, seated himself on the footstool at Margaret's knees, and, taking her dainty hand, said :

'I suppose you were surprised to see me, Madge, eh?'

'No; we have been expecting you for some time. I thought you would come at Christmas.'

'Why, what made you think that, Madge?'

'Do you want me to tell you?' asked Margaret, in surprise.

'Upon my word I can't guess.'

'What made you come to-day?'

'Well, my love for you, I suppose.'

'Then did you not love me before?'

It was provoking to be tripped up by a girl in this manner. Roland was vexed at allowing himself to be caught. Somehow their hands separated without his observation. He knitted his hands over his knee, and, looking into the fire, replied to her question:

'Of course I loved you before, Madge—of course I did; but you remember I said I should not return for six months; that was my agreement with the old dad, which I was compelled to keep.'

'Then why have you broken it to-day?'

'Hang it all, Madge, you're not sorry to see me, are you?' asked Roland, petulantly.

'No, Roland,' she replied, gently.

'Then why do you badger me about with cross questions, and get me up in a corner like?'

Margaret rose from her seat without replying. Roland sprang up and took her hand.

'I beg your pardon, Madge. I have no right to speak to you in that manner. Pray sit down again. I have been awfully worried, and my temper is faulty.'

'Even your worries must not make you forget that you are speaking to a lady.'

A quick suspicion flashed upon Roland's guilty conscience that Margaret was pointing to the difference between herself and Folly.

'I promise you I will be more guarded,' he said. 'Believe me, Madge, nothing is further from me than the wish to slight you. I came with the best intentions in the world.'

Margaret was silent.

'Yes, I came with the fixed resolution to —that is, I came with the—in fact, the best resolution, and I—I—I wish you'd say something, Madge.'

'What do you wish me to say?'

'Well, I want you to tell me, in your nice, kind manner, you know, why you expected I should come at Christmas. That question is the obstacle that checks my flow of conversation.'

'I thought so because I believed that you really loved me, as you used to say, better than all the world.'

'Yes, Madge, that's beautiful to think of, and it's just like you to credit me with such a good heart. But then there was my father.'

'And here was I,' answered Madge, with a smile. Roland laughed too, feeling that he was now getting over the ground capitally.

'I see what you mean, Madge; that with the two before me I should not have hesitated as to which I should please. But you must remember that your own interests depended on my keeping my promise to the dad.'

'Do they not now?'

'Cornered again, by George!' Roland mentally exclaimed.

'Tell me, Roland,' said Madge, seriously, 'was it that consideration that prevented your coming?'

'I don't think that's a fair question.'

'Then I will not press it,' said Madge, sighing.

'No; let us return to the subject. You expected me on Christmas Day——'

'I was hardly reasonable, perhaps; but—'

'Oh, love and reason are not inseparable. Come, tell me all that you expected: I will forgive the inconsistency.'

'Then I expected that as you had neglected me two months for your pleasures, you would neglect your pleasures one day for me.'

'My pleasures!' said Roland, growing pale. 'How have I neglected you?'

'Is it not enough to be told that you have?'

For a moment Roland felt as if he must throw himself at Margaret's feet and tell her all; then it occurred to him that he could not throw up the defence he had begun, and he determined to brave it out.

'You refer to my letters. They grew fewer, I know. But then you cannot expect any rational being to continue writing six letters a week about nothing.'

'Love and reason in your case *are* inseparable.'

'You are just like Dick for hounding a fellow down with his own words, Madge. Come, do let us be amiable. You cannot surely think I ought to have written more than I did? What had I to tell you?'

'That's what I wanted to know, but couldn't find, from the letters you did send. Surely you would have more to say after being in London a month than you had on the first hour of your arrival; and yet the letter you sent me at that time would make twelve of the poor little scraps you have sent since. That was a manly letter that I will never part with; the last have been childish scrawls, that none save I would keep.'

'I am ashamed of them, Madge.' It was the first honest sentence he had spoken, and Margaret, catching the accent, smiled forgiveness; but he did not see it, he was looking straight into the fire, and, bent upon his suicidal plan of defence, continued, 'But there is this to be said in my excuse, I was aware of their folly, and that made the job difficult.'

Poor Margaret sighed again, and the hand she had extended to place in a loving caress among his fair curls fell upon her lap.

'Let us speak of your good intentions,' she said calmly. 'What are they?'

'I came expressly to ask you to be my wife at once.'

'That was very good of you,' she replied, with a little laugh.

Roland did not reply. He was thinking how Folly accepted his addresses without the critical analysation to which Margaret subjected them. It did not strike him that his addresses to her were not of a kind to provoke criticism. How on earth was he to get on with his duty if every word was made an obstruction? This cleverness of Margaret's was her one great fault—it was unfeminine. She should not forget that he was making a sacrifice for her. If he did not choose the happiest phrases to express his meaning, he at least could claim from her indulgence for his good intentions.

'You understand by my making this proposal before the term my father stipulated for that I am prepared to encounter his objection,' he said.

'Yes; you will go to him and say that you cannot fulfil your agreement, and must be permitted to act as if you were a man,' she replied, losing patience.

Roland gulped down the insinuation, and answered: 'Just so.'

'And if he insists upon having his own way, what then?'

'I am prepared to take an independent course.

'You have made up your mind how you will earn a living if he allows you to take an independent course ?'

'I shall hit upon some occupation, I dare say, although it is not exactly defined at present. Meanwhile, there is still something left of the money he gave me for us to go on with.'

'You would have to return it if you declined the conditions upon which he gave it,' she said.

Roland reflected that there might be very little of it to return. He had not looked at his banking account recently; but money had been flowing from him rapidly of late, he knew. He turned from the subject with impatience.

'Madge, you were not a bit frightened at the prospect of having to rough it when I proposed to you before.'

'I can still bear my burdens. It did not appear to me before that I might myself be a burden to you.'

'Oh, don't be afraid of that. I know my responsibilities, and am quite prepared to undertake them. Now, Madge, to the point —will you be my wife immediately in the face of all opposition ?'

'Yes, on one condition.'

'Speak; I'll be bound I can overcome any single difficulty you may suggest.'

'The condition is a very simple one. But you must first answer me one question from the very bottom of your heart—faithfully, honestly, truly. Answer me as you love me, as you respect yourself; answer me as if you were a boy again.'

'I will, Madge. I will answer you truly, as I hope to be forgiven for my sins,' he answered, in an earnest tone.

'Then I will be your wife—*if you wish it*. Now, Roland, answer as you hope for forgiveness. Do you want me to be your wife?'

It would have been easy to say 'Yes,' justifying the answer to his conscience afterwards by such sophistry as he had lately dealt in; but he felt it would be untrue. At that moment he did not wish to marry Margaret; and put to his honour he could not tell a lie, although it was expedient. Madge had touched the one sound chord in his heart, the only one which had not warped, and it responded with a true tone.

'No,' he said, in a low voice, quite different from that in which he had been speaking.

The simple word was more acceptable to Margaret than if he had clothed its sense in the most delicate euphemisms.

She rose and said, giving him her hand:

'That is the kindest word you have said to me, and banishes all the rest from my memory. It was the voice I love that spoke. Roland, I release you.'

CHAPTER VI.

A NEW PROSPECT.

WHEN Richard Vane opened the door of his study he heard no sound of voices. Walking into the sitting-room in his soft slippers unheard, he found his sister sitting with her hands in her lap looking into the fire, and alone. He guessed what had happened, and stood in silent pity for a moment; then he approached her.

She had shed tears; the face was pale and the eyes swollen that she turned to him.

She rose from her seat and came to meet him, and he took her in his arms as if he had been her father.

'Is it all over?' he asked gently, putting

his face against hers, as it rested against his shoulder.

'He loves me no longer, and he is gone,' she answered.

'He will return, finding that he can love none but you.'

'No; he has gone for ever.'

Richard did not attempt to convince her of what he felt at that moment to be the truth, knowing that he could not comfort her now by such an assurance. He sat down, taking Madge on his knee, and keeping his arm about her.

'I did not hear him go. I suppose he will sleep at the Hall,' said he.

Madge shook her head.

'He said he should be able to catch the last train to London.'

'Poor fellow!' murmured the vicar.

Margaret burst into tears.

'My poor Madge, thought he, 'you have reason to think he is gone for ever. What is to become of this young man, who seizes the moment of another's greatest distress as a fortunate occasion for his return to pleasure? Falling so quickly with duty as a curb, how quickly will he sink and how deep now that all restraint is removed! Where will his infatuation lead him? Will he become utterly worthless?'

He did not try to check Margaret's tears; she was the first to speak.

'It is as if he were dying; his simplicity and truth and kindly feeling are gone, and scarcely one feature remains unaltered of the Roland we loved. Can nothing be done to save him?'

'I hope so.'

The vicar spoke with thoughtful earnestness, and Margaret understood by his subsequent silence that the subject was not dismissed from his mind.

'Meg,' he said, after a while, 'the time has come for us to work. We have had a long holiday.'

'You know how grateful I shall be for an occupation now—that is why you propose it.'

'That is one consideration, indeed, but not the only one. The subject has been simmering in my mind for some time, and this last little spark brings it to boiling-point. Sit in the chair there, Madge, and let us discuss the matter in a business-like manner.'

Margaret left his knee, but she would not part with his hand.

'Do you remember in the summer-time telling me that I was too good for a vicar?'

'Yes; and so you are, Richard. Your theology is above the intelligence of the congregation, and your simple sermons that touch me so are wanted in a better place than Tangley. You are twenty times too good for a vicar, you ought to be a bishop.'

Richard laughed. His opinions of bishops was not of an exalted kind.

'At any rate,' said he, 'we are agreed that I am too good for a vicar, and so I shall resign my living.'

'Resign your living!' exclaimed Margaret, astonished.

'Yes, dear. I hope it will not grieve you deeply to leave the pleasant home?'

'Oh, Richard, it has been even less dear to me than to you. Think of your hollyhocks and your annuals.'

'I have thought of them and bidden them good-bye. I bade them farewell the day you were engaged, knowing that they would not bloom again for me.'

'And intended to leave the house when I was married. Oh, Dick, how selfish everyone is—except you! I never thought of the desolation you were to suffer.'

'You will make me vain, Madge.'

'Make *you* vain!' she exclaimed, and stopped short, looking at her brother through the tears that affection had brought to her eyes.

'So having made up my mind that I was too good for a vicar, I next came to the conclusion that a country hamlet was too circumscribed for my efforts.'

'So it is, dear. You should have a living in a great city, and write pamphlets for the leading Quarterlies. Where shall you go?'

'I think I will begin with St. Giles's; and my living will be the interest upon our little capital, with what we can get to help it out by teaching, or what not.'

'And you are going to give up writing, and all your delightful days among flowers and ferns, and a gentle life here for St. Giles's and hard work and mean fare?'

'Yes. I ask you to come with me, and to renounce as much.'

'It will be a grief to me, and I am a woman' (Roland marked that distinction); 'but what will it be to you?'

'A pleasure, if we work together and succeed. At least we will try to make it so.'

'But the quiet Sundays, and the little

birds, the fruit trees in the springtime, and the roses that you budded and were so proud of?'

'We shall find new happiness, Madge. And I was thinking that——'

'And this sweet old room. Do you remember when we had the windows open in the summer, and the wasps came humming in?'

'I dare say we shall be able to get a wasp or two in London, if you particularly want them. You did not love them much when they came upon the pie. You were more frequently calling upon me to slaughter the innocent creatures than to preserve them.'

'Shall you teach religion in the streets, Richard?' asked Margaret, following her own train of ideas.

'With a chair, and an umbrella, and a train of scrofulous young apostles? No, Meg, I don't think I shall teach anything more doctrinal than my Master taught. It will be enough if——'

'I wonder if the swallows will be suffered to build under the eaves when you are gone.'

'You are rude, Madge; you interrupt me. Will you listen to me, or shall I listen to you?'

'And you took such pains to fertilise the

garden in the autumn—just as if you were going to stay here all your life.'

'That was only fair to my successor.'

'What shall I be able to do?'

'That remains to be seen. A soldier does not know what part he is to take in the battle until he is in the field.'

'Your books, Richard, and our pictures and the piano,' said Margaret, looking round the room regretfully upon the household objects of her affection.

'We will take them with us—everything that is especially dear which we can take. We will not be as other fanatics, Madge; thinking it necessary to make ourselves wretched for the sake of virtue.'

'And when shall we begin the new life?'

'Quite soon. There is one hurrying to London now who claims our attention.'

'You will try to save Roland?'

'He must enter into the business of our lives.'

Margaret looked into the fire, musing.

'The snowdrops are already peeping above the ground on the sunny side of the cucumber frame.'

'They are very early visitors.'

'And soon the hedges will be dotted with

young buds, and then the pink bloom on the apple tree will begin to show. . . . Do you remember lying on the lawn beneath the apple tree there, in the hot summer afternoons, and the solemn old rooks flying homewards to their rookery in the still evening? . . .' Her chin twitched, and suddenly turning to the vicar she threw herself on his shoulder and burst into tears.

'Oh, my brother!' she cried, 'my heart is breaking, but whether with grief or with joy, I cannot tell.'

CHAPTER VII.

WIT AND WISDOM OF SIR ANDREW AVELING.

HE following morning Richard Vane walked to Aveling Hall, and obtained an interview with the baronet.

Sir Andrew Aveling could scarcely conceal the delight he felt in hearing that the engagement between his son and Margaret Vane existed no longer. He understood that delicacy required a semblance of regret in the presence of one who suffered collaterally from the estrangement; and he accordingly made his accent and countenance as mournful as he could when, after listening eagerly to the vicar's brief statement of facts, he said:

'Dear me! And so the engagement is absolutely broken, eh?'

'Absolutely,' replied the vicar, with a sigh.

'Well, well!' the baronet sighed responsively. Then, in a gloomy accent, 'I suppose he has been fascinated by some beautiful young lady in London now.'

'Yes; he has been fascinated by a very beautiful young actress.'

'This Folly, who is attracting so much attention? He said a great deal about her in his letters to me. Tut! tut! A very common young person, I'll be bound.'

'No. She seems to me a girl not at all of the ordinary kind.'

'You have seen her then—eh, my dear Vane?'

'Yes, I have seen her, and can perceive the attractions she would have for a young man of Roland's temperament.'

'Well now, you must admit, my dear fellow, that for once my judgment was right. I knew he would see the inadvisability of this match as soon as his eyes were opened to the fact that there was more than one pretty girl in the world.'

Richard Vane did not answer, did not attempt to set Sir Andrew right. Nothing was to be gained by showing him that his judgment had again been wrong, and that the result of opening Roland's eyes had been to take him to Tangley at once, with the express purpose of marrying Margaret. For something more than the small gratification of proving his own and his sister's superiority the vicar had come to Aveling Hall this morning.

Construing the vicar's silence to his own advantage, Sir Andrew continued:

'And though it is doubtless a most painful humiliation to poor Margaret—who has my sincere sympathy, I assure you—she has the consolation of knowing that had Roland's change of disposition occurred after his marriage with her, it would have been far worse for her and for all of us.'

Richard Vane let that pass, despite his own convictions, merely remarking that his sister would probably take advantage of what consolations the case offered.

'Poor girl! it is a terrible disappointment for her,' pursued the baronet. 'But you mustn't let her brood over it, Vane. Give her some occupation to divert her mind. That old vicarage is enough to curdle one's blood to look at this weather. Come, what can we do? I have it. Turn your service over to the curate for two or three months, and take the poor child down to the Mediterranean. You might do Rome at the same time, you know. Upon my honour, that's a capital idea. Do Rome, and when you come back let the people know what a devilish bad sort of place it is in a moral sense. Preach about the Pope and Romanism, and get up some anecdotes about the Vatican, and that sort of thing. I'll be bound it would make quite a small sensation in the village. People want working up now and then, and it has seemed to me for some time that your polemical discourses are a little heavy. If I were a young man that's just the sort of thing I should like to do. The change would be vastly beneficial to Margaret. Of course, my dear fellow, I need not say that the journey shall cost you nothing.' As he spoke, Sir Andrew laid his hand on his cheque-book, a panacea which, as a benevolent man, he kept constantly at hand when he sat in his library to receive casual visitors.

'I have no fears for my sister. She will recover without going so far as the Mediterranean for forgetfulness,' answered the vicar, in his self-composed, quiet manner; then, lifting his eyes from the ground, and looking full in Sir Andrew's face, he said: 'But what is to be done about Roland?'

'Roland! I am not anxious on his account now.' The last word escaped Sir Andrew involuntarily. 'What do you mean?'

'Now that the trial is ended there is no longer any necessity to expose him to temptation.'

Sir Andrew laughed lightly.

'I see what you are driving at. I forget you are a parson, Vane, when you wear that coat. Temptation! Ah, that's all right. Roland's not such a babe as you take him for. Let him have his fling, I say. I don't believe in that old idea of making young fellows good by coercion. He will be none the worse for seeing life. But I appreciate your motive in speaking, my dear fellow, and I thank you for it. Ah, the boy's all right.'

'Roland is impulsive and easily led. It is not fair to submit him to temptations which frequently even the strong fail to surmount.'

'A very proper remark of yours—very proper, indeed,' said Sir Andrew, feeling nettled that the vicar should presume to lecture him upon duty, as if he were a mere agriculturist. 'You must allow me, however, to know what is best to do in this case. Who should know so well as a father how to take care of his son? You will, if you please, let me use my own discretion here.'

Evidently the vicar was not willing to yield in this particular.

'I know Roland better even than you do,' he said; 'and I beg you to recall him from London. Send him to Rome, Egypt, anywhere, and it will save him. Let him see life, if you will, but show him the good as well as the bad side of it. In London he is in danger, and as you are the fittest person to save him, I ask you to do it.'

'Pooh! you talk rubbish. Stick to your sermons and your Sunday-schools, but leave me the management of my own affairs, if you please.' Sir Andrew waved his hands and shifted his chair to close the subject; but Mr. Vane was not to be shaken off.

'He has got into a loose set—a theatrical set——'

'Nonsense, sir! I wonder how you, a man of sense, can put faith in that effete notion. Of course it is your duty to condemn amusements and that sort of thing, but you know very well that the stage is not the sink of iniquity you reverend gentlemen represent it.'

'I do not wish to be unjust to any people, and I am not unjust in saying that members of the theatrical profession are loose in their opinions and behaviour.'

'You are altogether wrong. I hold them in the highest estimation. They are virtuous and respectable. It doesn't become you to speak lightly of those who elevate the tastes of the public, and whose vocation needs but the name of sacred to be equivalent with your own.'

'All that you say is quite just.'

'And I will maintain it!' cried Sir Andrew, striking the table with his fist in warm enthusiasm.

'I am glad to hear it. I admit that this young woman who has fascinated Roland may be as virtuous and worthy as my own sister; but I cannot think that she can ever be content with the quiet and sober life of a country lady, or that she will make Roland happy as his wife.'

'His wife! Great heavens! what are you talking about! His wife!— a common actress—a creature who dances half nude upon the public stage to amuse a crowd of idle, senseless, gaping fools!— a woman without reserve or delicacy, whom one would scorn to be seen beside in the open street !—a person who can scarcely claim the name of woman !— a mountebank—a posturante—a demi-rep—a——'

'Sir, I cannot listen to this abuse of one whom we have no reason to believe less honourable than others.'

'Others!—why they're all alike, and you know it, Vane. It's the cant of the age to talk about the dignified position of the stage and such rubbish, but we men of the world know exactly what these women are, and you insult me by supposing my son would stoop to marry one of them.'

'I see no escape, if you permit him to remain in London.'

'My son marry a woman of that kind, absurd ! He may be weak, and I admit that a child might guide him in ordinary affairs ; but where his honour is concerned—where the honour of his old father is touched—my dear boy, my dear Roland, can be firm. Marry a ballet-girl ! What on earth could have put that notion into your head ?'

'The fact that he loves her more than he loved my sister, whom he promised to marry.'

'Ah, that's an affair of another complexion.

The love for a good girl is very different from the passion for a merely beautiful woman : one necessitates marriage ; the other forbids it— but these are particulars which you are not supposed to know anything about.'

'But which I know, nevertheless. I know your meaning precisely ; it is that your son may love this girl without marrying her : that is a disgrace which must never befall Roland.'

'Mr. Vane,' said Sir Andrew, rising, 'we will close this discussion before you provoke me to anger. Neither my son nor I stand in need of direction where our honour is concerned. I will not go over what you have said, or point out in what particulars you affront me. They are too obvious to call for remark. When you tell me that my son is likely to marry a posturante you affront me ; you add another insult by presuming that my son is liable to fall into disgrace ; another, when you attempt to dictate rules for my conduct ; and still another by mentioning the subject at all ; and, confound it, sir, I won't listen to another word !'

The vicar sat unmoved, while Sir Andrew, pacing up and down the library, dilated on those points which he had declared it unnecessary to refer to. He saw that nothing was to be done with the intractable and inconsistent old man, and he gave up the hope of his co-operation with little disappointment: he had not expected much assistance from him. All that could be done he must do himself, and without delay. He waited patiently for the baronet's excitement to abate before broaching the second subject. This silence aggravated Sir Andrew, despite his assertion that he would not listen to another word.

'Hang it all, Vane!' he cried, 'why don't you say something? You know very well that nothing is dearer to me than discussing my boy's welfare; and who can advise me so well as you, who know the secrets of his heart? There are a thousand things that a boy tells his friend which he conceals from his father. And who has a greater right to speak in his behalf than you, who saved his life? Believe me, I never forget that and the debt of gratitude I owe you.'

'I have said all that I can say on the subject, Sir Andrew, and I hope that, when you reflect calmly on the matter, you will see the advisability of withdrawing Roland from London.'

'Ah, there, my dear Vane, I cannot agree with you, and shall not if I reflect until doomsday; but on any other point you will find me most amenable to your advice.'

'I have nothing else to advise. A second purpose I had, however, in coming here to-day.'

'Name it, Richard. All you ask shall be granted without question, I promise.'

'I wish to resign my living.'

'That I'll never consent to. Resign your living—why, for Heaven's sake!'

'For Heaven's sake I must,' answered Vane, with a faint smile.

'You are not offended at anything I might have said in the heat of argument, Vane? For if you are, you will make me regret that ever I spoke at all. There's no one I respect so much as you—no one.'

The impulsive, soft-hearted old gentleman spoke with honest warmth, and held out his hand with an action of entreaty. Richard Vane took it and pressed it.

'It is not temper, but conscience which directs me now.'

'You can't digest the Thirty-nine Articles, eh? Well, who can? You must do as the rest of the parsons do—that is, those who have any sense in their heads—bolt 'em, and forget 'em.'

'I am troubled with something heavier than the Articles.'

'I know—Joshua and the sun—Noah's ark—the Red Sea business—and all that, eh? Well, well; you must find out how wise and good men reconcile the contradictory facts of science and revelation and do likewise, satisfying yourself with the reflection that you are no worse than others.'

'My conscience is of an obstinate and unaccommodating nature. I cannot take money under false pretences without feeling myself dishonest to men, and I cannot teach a doctrine in which I have no faith, without dishonesty to God."

'Bah, Vane! These are the qualms which a young conscience feels when it first embarks upon the sea of speculation. You will recover, and sail along comfortably enough after a while.'

'I have doubted, but now I doubt no longer. I have set aside speculations—I have done with them. My laboured arguments to prove wrong right you have listened to every Sunday since I accepted my vicarship——'

'And capital good sermons they have been, too. I never heard better. The reasoning is most profound, and the sentences beautifully rounded.'

'They have cost me much useless labour. The little I have done to make men true and good has come spontaneously from me. To say and do what I know to be true and good —that is how I must serve God. I have to teach not philosophy, but religion.'

'Give us a little of both, morning and evening, as you have used to. Variety is good. We could never get a better man than you. Does not that fact satisfy you?'

'No. I am not justified in giving little because much is not a compulsory requirement of my office. I can do more good out of the Church than in it—at least I hope so. I must give all that I can, and sink my own temporal interests in the one endeavour to do that which God tells me I should do.'

'Ah, well!' replied the baronet, shrugging his shoulders and flinging himself back in his chair.

* * * *

When Richard Vane was gone, Sir Andrew sat for some time reflecting on the particulars of the interview.

He felt mingled admiration and contempt for the vicar. High principles, steadfastness, and that sort of thing were very proper and admirable, of course; but that a man, for a mere conscientious fad, should renounce such substantial blessings as ease and comfort seemed to him sheer folly and Quixotism.

He considered Vane as a dreamer—which of all things he least was—a man who formed eccentric notions of things—a man to be admired but not imitated. He classed him with those over-nice people who must analyse their drink before they satisfy their thirst; finikin, troublesome people, who generally end by poisoning themselves with the particular venom they have sought to avoid.

It seemed to him that Vane's view of Roland's little affair was not less extravagant than the aspect he put upon his own moral obligations. Who but such a man as he would think that a love affair with a ballet-girl must end in marriage, or look upon a little wildness as a desperate sin? So long as Roland was safe, what was there to fear?

He was heartily sorry that the vicar should have fallen into an error which must inevitably lead him into trouble. The radical principles he betrayed would prevent his rising to any decent position in society, and might reduce him to the rank of common reformers and agitators. That terrible possibility, painful as it was to think of, served to increase the satisfaction with which he regarded his son's escape from an alliance with the vicar's sister.

His greatest fear was that Roland might be touched with remorse, compassion, or some such absurd sentiment, which would bring him again under the influence of Margaret. To prevent such a disaster Sir Andrew saw that the young man must be encouraged in his wildness, and have his fling without impediment or restriction. Accordingly he wrote at once to congratulate him upon escaping a *mésalliance*, and hinted that if his resources were at all straightened he might draw upon him for his further requirements.

CHAPTER VIII.

ROLAND'S FLING.

'SOWING wild oats,' 'Running wild,' 'Having a fling,' these are the terms in which we refer to a young man's indulgence in sensuous excesses. By most people it is regarded as an indispensable disease of manhood—like the distemper of puppies, which they must go through with and get over before they arrive at perfection. To youths and puppies we are indulgent at these times, and if they bite we forgive.

It is understood that when a young man is having his fling he gives himself up, body and soul, to wild delight with a dashing, devil-may-care gaiety which knows no control.

It may be interesting to know how near to

this conception Roland approached as he played his part in the performance sanctioned by his father.

Twelve o'clock has struck. For the last quarter of an hour the waiters at 'The Nocturnal' have been praying the visitors to depart. Roland and Folly are the last to leave.

'What a brutal shame it is to turn people out into the streets at this hour? I am just beginning to wake up; and now what are we to do?' Roland asks, pulling the collar of his ulster up.

'Go home,' answers Folly, with a laugh.

Roland shrugs his shoulders.

They stand in the vestibule outside the supper-room, Folly muffled up to her chin in soft rich furs. Her pretty, saucy little face attracts a good deal of attention from the young men loitering there.

'Brougham, miss?' says Folly's driver, coming towards them.

'I hate that four-wheeled cab; let's have the hansom, Folly,' says Roland.

The girl responds with a little gesture of indifference.

Roland nods to a quick-eyed, knowing-looking fellow, standing in the background, who wears round his throat a silk handkerchief with Roland's monogram embroidered in the corners.

The driver of the brougham touches his hat and departs, and presently Roland, giving his arm to Folly, leads her out to the hansom, which has drawn up to the door. The man who put his coat over the cab-wheel as Folly stepped in, and closed the door afterwards, gets half-a-crown for his service, and the hansom dashes off.

'If it were not such a horrid night I would make you go for a long drive with me before parting. It's hateful when you are gone,' says Roland.

Folly looks into his face with a sweet smile, for him to interpret as he pleases, then shrinks back into the corner, nestling her chin down in her furs. For all her seeming indifference, she prefers the hansom to the brougham; it is the swifter vehicle, and from the moment she came off the stage she has begrudged the time spent in Roland's society. She is anxious about her father, and eager to return to the imbecile old man. For this reason she is glad that the weather is too bad to admit of an extended ride.

A glimpse of Folly's bright eyes when

they approach a lamp, the touch of her dress, the consciousness that she is beside him— that is all the satisfaction Roland gets from the drive. Conversation is impossible, for the roads, after leaving the Strand, are bad; he has to shout to make himself heard, and the necessity of keeping her mouth covered limits Folly's response to two indefinite muffled sounds which represent the words 'Yes' and 'No.'

'What an infernal place this is to live in!' says Roland, as they reach the Lambeth Road. 'If those diamonds hadn't crippled me, I would furnish a house for you to-morrow.'

Folly takes her muff from her mouth, and pats his arm with it.

The hansom stops. The driver gets down from his seat, and, running up to the door of the house, knocks. There is a light on the first floor. Across the white blind there passes the shadow of a bent, high-shouldered old man, with a round head and hideous face, its proportions exaggerated and still further distorted by the position of the light behind. A corner of the blind is stealthily drawn aside.

'Father is awake; you mustn't get out,' says Folly.

A chill runs through Roland's body as he pictures Folly submitting to the caresses of that revolting old wretch she insists upon regarding as her father. For the moment she seems to him tainted with the breath of the loathsome idiot.

Miss Clip opens the street-door, and the driver returns to the hansom.

'You will come for me at six to-morrow?' says Folly.

'Won't you dine with me? It is not right for you to be so much with that old man. I wish to Heaven you would let me place him in a proper asylum!'

Had anyone else spoken, Folly would have answered indignantly, 'What asylum is more proper for my father than my home?' but she has learned to conceal her real feelings and simulate false sentiments in Roland's presence.

'He is rather horrid; and there's a nice large building close by,' she said lightly, referring to Bethlehem Hospital—a place she never passed but with averted eyes. 'We must see about getting rid of him when I have my new house. Good-night.'

Folly runs up to the house—turning, when she is out of the vision of the old man at the window, to wave her hand to Roland. The door closes behind her, and the last spark of cheerfulness in Roland's heart goes out; his soul seems leaden, and heavy, and dead, like the humid night.

The driver takes his seat and turns the cab. Looking through the side window, Roland sees the old man still stealthily watching by the drawn blind, and by his side the shadow of Folly, her hand resting on his arm.

Roland has never thought what the logical outcome of his passion for Folly will be; he has no scheme for the future; he lives as he has always lived—for the hour. But a vague consciousness that he is incurring a grave responsibility, that the thread of his destiny is getting inextricably tangled with Folly's, a dim presentiment that he must get into a desperate scrape before long, oppresses him, increasing the morbid wretchedness he feels in solitude. He thinks of Margaret and the serenity of his happiness when his heart was entirely hers. He shakes off these reflections to think of something different. He can fix his mind on nothing but the story in the 'Arabian Nights' of Sindbad burdened with the clinging old man of the sea. He pictures the old man toothless, and bald, and mad, like Folly's father. He has just passed over Kennington Road. A cart against the pavement is being unloaded. What is the dark object the men are lifting out at this time of night? He looks until, drawing closer, he sees it is a coffin being taken into the dead-house of Bethlehem Hospital. He shuts his eyes with a feeling of sickness.

'Kensington, sir?' asks the driver through the trap.

'Yes, as sharp as you can.'

Roland feels a craving for fresh sparkling wine, of which there is plenty in his chambers. Yet the thought of the dark empty room is repulsive. It is impossible to go to bed yet; he shall not be able to sleep; he cannot read—what the deuce shall he do? It will be better to go to the Corinthus and play loo, though he hates cards, and is rather afraid of the men he meets at the club. But he will find there at least light and warmth, and some sort of diversion for his mind. He thrusts up the trap over his head and gives the driver fresh instructions.

Roland has been a member of the Corinthus two months. Amadis Garnier, who is member of half-a-dozen clubs, put his name up and introduced him, giving him a word of caution at the same time.

'The men are prigs,' said he, 'and decidedly fast; but their bounce is amusing, and you are not bound to go to the deuce by the path *they* choose. If you want a good dinner, a good cigar, or decent wine, you can get it here.'

The Corinthus is sufficiently near Pall Mall to be respectable. It is a young club, composed of young men titled without money and young men moneyed without title. Money or rank is an indispensable qualification. Roland has found it useful to him on many occasions, and the members, though bumptious, and swaggering, and pretentious, and fast, as Garnier intimated, are courteous and civil enough to him. He only suspects that they laugh at him, and criticise his private affairs in an unfriendly manner behind his back. No one ever refuses to dine with him or pleads business engagements when he proposes to drink champagne.

It is a rule of the club that the doors shall never be closed. No restrictions are imposed upon members using the card-room—an arrangement which gives freedom to the inclination, precludes the necessity of resting at ordinary times, and affords a relief from the *triste* conventionalities of society.

At the club-house entrance Roland steps out of the hansom, and, putting a few cigars into the driver's hand, says, 'I dare say I shall be half an hour; you may wait for me.'

The cabman touches his hat, and, knowing Roland better than Roland knows himself, makes arrangements for a lengthened stay. First he throws a cloth over his horse's loins, next he buckles on the nosebag, and then, like a merciful man, having provided for the comfort of his beast, he steps into the cab, wraps a second cloth about his legs, lights a cigar, and, crossing his arms, composes himself comfortably in the corner.

As dear as salvoes of artillery to the heart of a prince is the popping of corks to Roland's ears. It is to him a guarantee of his friends' fidelity—a fidelity which of late, in his gloomy and sombre moments, he has got to doubt uneasily. In the smoking-room are half-a-dozen of these friends about the fire, and all prove themselves again ready to stand by him and drink at his expense. The light wine does him all the good he anticipated from it—showing how one's instincts are to be trusted in such matters. It freshens him, and dispels his melancholy. Champagne is certainly the best of medicine, he considers, and argues that if one bottle is good, two must be better. He is quite ready to engage in pool when it is proposed; he likes the billiard board.

He plays, and keeps his hand in with frequent drinks, until he loses 'form,' and finds the room inconveniently hot. The idea of going home is still repulsive to him, and he himself suggests an adjournment to the card-room, and a cool game at nap. His friends are the most amiable men in the world, and fall in with his suggestion at once.

In the card-room he begins with drinking; he drinks while he plays, and when he can puzzle out the difference between ace and deuce no longer he drinks again, and is helped into the hansom by his friends and the cabman. He has lost fifty, a hundred, two hundred pounds—it matters little which, his good friends are the gainers by it. When the time comes for paying up it will appear that they were all a little the worse for drink when they played, and so—the chances being equal—the debt will stand good, with no question of any dishonourable advantage being taken on either side.

It is six o'clock when he shuffles off his clothes and crawls into bed. He sleeps fitfully until one, when a ray of sunlight falling on his face awakens him, and discovers the suggestive fact that he went to bed without drawing down the window-blind. He rises to draw it down now and see what the deuce he did with his watch. The watch is safe in his waistcoat pocket: he finds it among the heap of clothes on the floor; it has stopped —that's all. Conscious that he does not feel quite right, Roland determines to take a little dose of something and go to bed again for an hour. He keeps drugs in the cupboard where his wine is stowed away—enough quack medicines to stock a shop. There they are— bane in large bottles at the bottom, antidote in small vials at the top. Looking at the many infallible cures, he is doubtful which to take. The tonic he tried yesterday, and derived no benefit from it; but whether to try the corrective, which is for the stomach, or the elixir, which ministers to a liver diseased, is a question that is difficult to answer, as he is not certain, in the general feeling of his discomfort, which part of his anatomy is at fault. In this condition of uncertainty he takes a bottle from the bottom of the cupboard, and treats his disease by the homœopathic rule. Then, recollecting the admirable effects of Richard Vane's treatment, he wraps a wet towel round his head, and so gets into bed again.

By half-past two Roland is dressed and waiting for his breakfast. He sits with his legs thrust out, his hands buried in his trousers pockets, his chin on his breast, and a hang-dog expression on his face. Those who *will* be gay overnight may expect this kind of thing in the morning. There is a glass opposite. Raising his head, he catches sight of his yellow skin and leaden eyes. He turns his chair round in disgust, and fixes his vacant gaze upon an antimacassar, until the yellowness of it makes him feel ill.

'Why the deuce doesn't the woman bring the breakfast?' he cries, crossing the room in angry haste to jerk the bell violently. He is not hungry. If the most tempting morsel were at his hand he could not put it to his lips. He has forgotten all about the breakfast before it is laid upon the table. Throwing himself upon a couch with the first book he touches, he opens the page and tries to read, but the words have no meaning for him and the type tries his eyes. He throws the book away petulantly, and, knitting his fingers under his head, stares up at the ceiling, finding faces in the cracks that run across. Is there any face like Margaret's there? No, nothing half so sweet. How is it he cannot forget her, now that the engagement is all over and she has released him? The flowing line seems to him like the ripple of her hair when they were children, and went into the hazel wood for nuts. Why should he think of that time, and remember only her hair? Was there not a beautiful ripple in Folly's tresses? No; his thoughts return to Margaret. Ought he—might he —think of her now? He could call her Madge never again. The old tie is broken, even the old friendship is ended. What should he do if he met her by accident? Should he bow and pass? Would she hold out her hand to him in forgiveness, or would they pass as though they were strangers? Would dear old Dick forgive him, or had he overtaxed even his patience? Surely he must be scorned by the quiet, holy brother and sister. Perhaps that was why Richard had not written to him or taken any further notice of him. And if Vane repudiated him, would not all decent men look down on him with contempt? Following the crack in the ceiling, his eye travelled to an irregular deviation from the rippling line, which formed a huge distorted mouth, with a dark spot like a black tooth standing out from the lower jaw. It was a little like the shadow on the blind as Folly's father approached the window. That creature must be his companion, must take the place of pure, healthy Richard Vane, his old friends of the university: Bowles, studying for the bar, and Renfrew, with his stories of travel and adventure, and the high-born, delicate Raby Seymour—these and other clear-minded, Christian gentlemen must be forgotten, and his associates must be the men of the Corinthus, who fleeced him and let him go wrong without a word of remonstrance. And Margaret—Madge, with her lively fancies, her refined manners, her delicate tastes, her graceful manners and appearance—who is to take her place?

'Folly!' he answers, springing up in excitement.

She comes before his eyes in all her glowing colours. He can see nothing else; he wants to see no more. To think of others makes him wretched and low-spirited; she gives him joy, and makes him forget all care. He could not live if she should go from his world. She is the world to him. The love of father and friends sinks into insignificance as he recalls Folly's smile. That memory transports him with delight, and he looks forward with intense eagerness to meeting her again. He pulls out his watch to see how the hours creep; the hands still point the time at which it stopped.

This turn of sentiment, though but a mere reactionary wave, has removed the feeling of nausea with which he previously regarded the breakfast-table, and he turns to it now with an idea that he could eat a little dry toast. His father's letter lies beside the cup. He breaks the envelope, and sits down before reading the letter, fearful that Sir Andrew has heard all from Vane and writes in anger. What if the old gentleman should demand an account of his expenses, and refuse any further supplies? Roland has expected every day to receive an intimation from his bankers to the effect that his account is overdrawn. He opens the letter slowly, and looks at the first words in apprehension. 'My dear boy.'

He gives a sigh of relief. There is no anger in those words. He reads on quick and yet quicker.

'What an old trump!' he says, coming to the conclusion.

On the face of it the letter is encouraging. His father does not condemn him, nor disapprove of his *liaison*. On the contrary, he offers the means for a continuance of his present mode of living.

Then he goes through it again with increased satisfaction, and afterwards, holding the letter in his hand, ponders what he has read. It is difficult to thoroughly understand all that his father means. He opens the letter a third time.

After congratulating him upon avoiding a *mésalliance* with Margaret Vane, Sir Andrew writes: 'Your escape at this moment is especially fortunate, as poor Vane has been seized with some preposterous notion of a dangerously Radical kind, and is resigning his living, to gain a subsistence by what means Heaven only knows. It would not astonish me to hear soon of his stumping the country in the character of a revivalist or a demagogue. You could not have held your position as a country gentleman with a connexion of that kind, and I need not point out to you the serious domestic complications which would have arisen in consequence, *had* you been so unwise as to carry out your intention of marrying Vane's sister.'

'It is odd Dick said nothing of this to me,' thinks Roland. 'I wonder what he will do? I only hope he won't come to London.'

'I have heard of your infatuation for the pretty actress now creating such a sensation in London,' the letter continues. 'You must bear in mind that people of that kind are dangerous if you permit them to cross that line of demarcation which separates them from our class of society. While you remember that Folly forms part of a public exhibition you are safe.'

'Vane blurted out everything, then, to the dad,' Roland remarks, parenthetically.

'I have no faith in restriction. I have been a young man myself, and had my own experiences. I leave you to do entirely as you please, without even offering my advice. You will understand, my dear boy, that while I desire you shall do nothing derogatory to your honour, I put no limit to your enjoyment of life and of those indulgences which enable young men to know men and women as they are divested of that glamour which frequently betrays them with false sentiment, and leads them to perpetrate mistakes that may be a source of life-long regret.'

And then follows the paragraph sanctioning Roland to draw upon his father for more money if he requires it.

The baronet's meaning is clear, yet it takes Roland some time to comprehend its full extent. When he does he is bewildered. It is to him like a revelation of something he has never dreamed of. He blushes to the temples like a girl—not for himself, but for his father.

Roland is as yet guiltless of any deliberate wickedness. He has yielded to circumstances only, not moulded them to a base purpose. He cannot think without repulsion of breaking down the delicate fabric of modesty with which he has clothed Folly.

'My father has mistaken her—that is excusable; but he has also mistaken me; and does me wrong,' he thinks.

Nevertheless, within an hour—so speedily does an ill seed take root in a soil suitably prepared—he reads his father's letter for the last time with a different feeling, and, concluding it, asks, 'After all, who has been mistaken—he or I?'

CHAPTER IX.

GOOD NEWS.

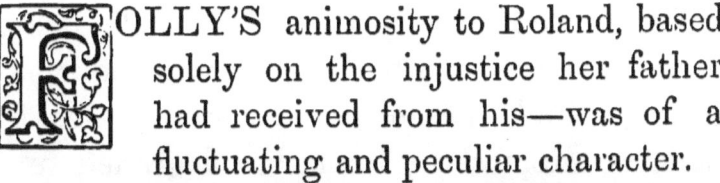

OLLY'S animosity to Roland, based solely on the injustice her father had received from his—was of a fluctuating and peculiar character.

In her calmer moments, or when Roland was particularly kind, and so fortunate as to avoid saying anything that touched her suspicious sensitiveness, she hated him less from a spontaneous feeling than from a sense of duty—vengeance seemed to her a filial obligation. It was impossible for one of her generous disposition to cherish a mean passion, which can dwell only in very bad hearts or unemotional minds. But for her pet paragraph from the Mosaic law she would have acknowledged to herself the wrongness of revenge, and the injustice of visiting the father's sin upon the son.

It was another thing, however, when she was with her father, listening to the broken story of his life. He talked of nothing else, having found by experience that she would yield more readily to his entreaties for a dram when her heart was moved with compassion for his past sufferings. At these times no thought of mercy softened her passionate anger. She wanted only the power to sweep the Avelings, father and son, from off the face of the earth. Her whole being was stirred with a barbaric craving for vengeance; and she gloated over the idea of sending Roland to his father degraded and loathsome, as her father had come to her. Her scheme of reducing him by champagne was something like storming a fortress with pop-guns, but it was the only plan that her girlish mind could devise; she was not a Borgia. In her passions she was merely a savage.

Like some savages, it was necessary to foster her vengeful feelings by the sight of ancient scars and the hearing of her tribe's traditionary wrongs. Without these external incentives the hatchet had been buried.

There were several reasons why she should like Roland—he was generous, he loved her, he did as she desired him to do, and, above all, he treated her with respect. There was a deference in his behaviour to her which she received from none other of the many gentlemen introduced to her, although they got less encouragement than he. He treated her as though she were a lady and his equal, and that convinced her that he was a gentleman. She knew he was considered a fool, 'a muff, with more wealth than wit,' and so on, but since his foolishness consisted in treating her so well she could not like him less for it.

Her moods varied with the disposition of her father. If he had a 'bad time' during the day, Roland knew it at night-time by her coldness and unwillingness to meet him early the next day; if she was amiable and complying, he knew that her father had not troubled her. He did not know the fundamental reason for her altering manner towards him: he attributed it solely to her filial solicitude, and found in that a sufficient explanation of her behaviour.

On the night succeeding his receipt of Sir Andrew's letter he found Folly in her best humour. Her father had slept all the afternoon, and awoke just as she was about to depart for the theatre.

'You don't look well, Roland, she said, almost regretfully, comparing his present unhealthy appearance with the fresh brightness of his face when she first knew him, and reflecting that he owed the alteration to her.

'I was fool enough to play until I couldn't see out of my eyes. The old complaint, Folly, and the old remedy—loss of you, and excitement to forget the loss.'

'Poor fellow!' she said, laying her hand on his arm with the instinctive sympathy of a woman for a man in trouble.

He caught her hand, and, holding it tightly, looked into her soft eyes as he had never looked before, except when he was drunk; and now he was sober.

'I never can be happy living apart from you,' he said.

She snatched her hand away, laughing lightly, the hansom stopping at that moment before the stage-door.

Roland was excited by his own boldness; he caught hold of her arm as they threaded their way through the dusky intricacies of the *coulisses*—an unnecessary assistance he had not offered before—and parted with it reluctantly at the foot of the stairs leading to the dressing-rooms. He stood looking after her as she ran up, hoping she would turn around.

'Folly!' he cried, when she was almost at the top of the stairs.

'Well?' she replied, stopping and looking down on him.

'Look sharp down. I have good news to tell you—a letter from the governor. You will find me in the shrubbery.'

She nodded and ran up; and Roland made his way to the shrubbery—a facetious name given to the snug green-room of the Levity.

'What an ass I was to tell her I had the letter!' he said to himself. 'She will want me to read it to her. I must make an excuse to avoid that.'

Roland could no more keep a secret than a sieve can hold water, and it was characteristic of his impetuous desire to please that he repeatedly had to repent one moment of something he had done the previous minute.

He had resolved, before seeing Folly, that he would not let her know of that letter from his father, but the delicate consideration which led him to form the resolution gave way to bolder desires as he stood looking up the stairs after the beautiful girl. Now he regretted the mistake, wondering how he could remedy it.

Folly took little time to dress; she had not to make up her face—at any time she could lean her cheek upon her pale kid gloves without altering the tint of either. No one but Roland was in the shrubbery when she came down.

'Well, what is your good news?' she asked, sitting down beside Roland, and breaking the string that tied her parcel of new gloves.

'Not much—only the governor approves of what I have done.'

'Approves of your breaking off the engagement with Miss Vane?'

'Yes.'

'Why?'

'Well, you see he didn't think it would be a good match for me. I told you that he did not like my engagement.'

'You didn't tell me why. How did I know he disliked it on your account?—it might have been upon hers,' said Folly, naïvely.

'No; he thought I might do better.'

'You told me she was a good girl—didn't he think so?'

'Yes. No one could doubt that. But he

thought that possibly after I had married her I should see some one I should like better.'

Folly looked puzzled for a moment. Then, as an idea came to her mind, she said:

'I see—he thought you would see some one prettier. That's very likely. I should think the sister of that man I saw after the ball couldn't be very much to look at.'

'Still she is pretty—very pretty and graceful indeed—but not so beautiful as you, Folly.'

'If your father is a sensible old gentleman,' said Folly slowly, as she pulled on her long glove, 'I can't see how he should think you could do better than marry a girl that was pretty and graceful and good. Fasten these buttons for me.'

'My father has peculiar ideas about some things—I don't think you could quite understand them!'

'Yes, I shall, if you explain them.'

'What a lovely round arm yours is, Folly!'

'Yes; but about these ideas of your father's?'

'Well, my father is a justice of the peace —a sort of magistrate.'

'Yes, I know; a rich man who sends poor men to prison—eh?'

'Something like that, indeed,' Roland admitted, with a laugh.

He was bending over the pretty arm, and could not see the evil in Folly's eyes as she looked at his smiling face.

'He was a member of Parliament,' said Roland.

'What's that?'

'One who assists in making laws for the protection of life and property.'

'I understand—laws for their own protection.'

'Not entirely for themselves.'

'Why?—poor men who have no property, and whose lives are a burden to them, need no protection.'

Again Roland laughed at the conceit.

'You're quite a Republican,' he said.

'What's that?'

'A Republican?—oh, a discontented person, who would throw over existing laws to substitute those which *he* thinks more just.'

'What do you call such a person?'

'A Republican.'

'A Republican,' said Folly, repeating the word to herself, as if to impress it on her mind; then she added, in a voice tinged with contempt, 'So your father is a justice of the peace and was a member of Parliament—well?'

'I'm sorry to say I have finished this glove. May I do the other?'

She gave him the other glove to fasten, saying:

'Be quick, and tell me about your father. I shall be called before you get to the good news.'

'I was saying that my father, holding this position, is proud of it, and values the respect of the county families above everything. Well, he has a notion that when I attain to his age I must have the same feelings, and that then I should regret having married Margaret when I might have married some one better—I mean higher in position—a girl of a noble family, you know. In a moral sense, I couldn't marry anyone better than Margaret.'

'Then you have the same idea, and that is why you gave up Margaret?'

'No, it was not that; I gave her up—or rather she gave me up—because——'

He paused, looking hastily round the room. It was empty. Seldom anyone came into it until after the first act, and the first act had only just begun.

'Because—why?'

Roland transferred his quivering fingers from her glove to her soft arm, and said, in a low, impassioned voice :

'Because I love you, Folly. It is useless for me to cheat myself with the idea that I only admire you and love you as one may love a friend or a child. I love you with all my heart, as a man loves a woman.'

Folly's heart was not stirred by reciprocal emotion. She had no love for Roland; she knew nothing of the passion by experience; she had seen it acted upon the stage, and this was to her but a little play, in which she took the part of heroine. She looked at Roland's flushed cheeks and dilated pupils coldly enough.

'Folly, don't you understand me? Haven't you seen that I deceived myself in treating you merely as a friend? Don't you know that I love you? Don't you see what has deranged my senses and made me your slave? You know what love is. You are not a child.'

'And do you really love me?' asked Folly.

He tried to express in words the passion that agitated his breast. His tongue failed him; he looked down at the arm he still held in his hands, and, lifting the beautiful down-covered limb to his lips, he pressed eager kisses upon it for an answer.

'Miss Folly called!' cried the call-boy, thrusting in his head at the open door.

CHAPTER X.

A PROPOSAL.

THE manager of the Levity was not strict in enforcing the regulation pasted on the notice-board at the stage-door—'No person allowed to pass the stage-door unless absolutely engaged in the performance.'

As a matter of fact any person who spent money freely at the Levity was permitted to pass the stage-door, and could take a friend with him occasionally. The manager saved considerably in the salaries paid to the ladies of his company by this arrangement, obtained the friendship of newspaper critics, and could evade the Jews if a failure compelled him suddenly to raise money.

From the stage-door there were two passages; one that led to the green-room, the other leading to the business part of the stage. The regulation on the notice-board literally referred to this latter passage; it was barred to all save employés after the performance had commenced. The manager was a shrewd man of business, and while he conceded the green-room to his patrons and friends, excluded them rigorously from the wings where their presence would interfere with the business of the stage. After the curtain had risen, not even Roland, who was as well known behind the scenes as the manager himself, could pass the commissionaire who guarded the communication between the green-room and the wings. Thus he was parted from Folly when she ran away in answer to the summons of the call-boy.

Knowing that Folly would not return until the close of the act, and unable to sit still in his present condition of feverish restlessness, he left the theatre, made his way down one of the turnings from the Strand to the Embankment, where he walked, trying in vain to think composedly of what he had done and what must ensue. All that he could think of was Folly's arm and how it yielded to his lips. He bit the end of his cigar through and through, and fretted it away with his teeth, while his fingers twisted and rolled the edges of the letters in his pockets into pellets. He reckoned it would take him a quarter of an hour to get back to the theatre, and to be in time he started to return five-and-twenty minutes before the act would conclude. He made the distance in seven minutes.

A couple of men had come into the green-room and were looking at the portraits in the album on the table. Roland wished them anywhere else; how could he make love to her before these men and the members of the company who would leave the stage with her? The difficulty had not presented itself to his mind before.

One of the men he knew well—Delaunay, a member of the Corinthus; the other was Delaunay's friend, a young viscount, and the son of a statesman well known for his culture and high morality. This young man had the misfortune to resemble in some features the hero of a popular authoress; he was large, stupid, and a guardsman. Being proud of the resemblance, he was now doing his best to supply those deficiencies in which nature fell short of the demi-rep's ideal. He was wicked less from natural inclination than a perverted sense of duty, basing his contempt for virtue on the dogma maintained by another hero of his authoress, stated in these words, ' It is very *bourgeois* to do right.'

Delaunay introduced his friend and opened the conversation. What they said was not worth repeating, being the reverse of George Eliot's definition of sarcasm ; it was indecency without wit, and repulsive enough to any clean ear. The young nobleman did most of the talking; Roland most of the listening. Such talk he had heard many times before, and considered the ridicule of honour and decency as a merely idle and nasty fashion, like the sucking of toothpicks, and not as the sincere avowal of a general principle. But now he listened with ears differently attuned, and took their words and meaning to be the same. A few weeks before if anyone had laid down the proposition that morality was an old-fashioned virtue, for which there was no longer any necessity, Roland would have opposed it with all the strength of his honest convictions, but now he said nothing ; indeed he rather doubted if after all there was not some truth in the argument.

It is thus that we allow ourselves to be influenced by men whose opinions we have despised, and take them for our leaders when they go the way that we would go.

His reflections were broken by the chorus which formed the *finale* to the first act. Over the united voices of the other singers and the full accompaniment of the orchestra he could hear Folly's voice ringing clear and high. The last bar was lost in the roar of applause which ceased only when the chorus was repeated. Again plaudits mingled with the concluding notes, and shortly afterwards the door opened quickly and Folly entered flushed and panting, with eyes that rivalled the diamonds on her neck in glittering brilliancy. Behind her came the low comedians and the *jolies petites* of the company, all chattering and laughing like children let out of school. There is always something to talk about at the conclusion of an act, and everyone has something to say about it, which is of such paramount importance that it must be said in a very high voice and very quickly.

Folly loved her business and 'talked shop' like an old actress, and it was five minutes before she could settle down to any other consideration, though Roland stood at her elbow, and the matter she had to discuss with the low comedian was of a most trivial kind. Then Delaunay came up, introducing his friend, who engaged her for another five minutes in listening to flattery of a personal sort, witless enough, and only redeemed from *bourgeois* simplicity by its intended rudeness. These attentions Folly received night after night from one or another, and regarded as carelessly as the comments of the dirty denizens of the court she passed through to the stage-door. Roland stood by, moody and silent. The impertinencies were more objectionable to his ear than they had been before, and he was hurt to think that Folly had no more consideration for him than to listen patiently to such stuff at that time.

'Have you forgotten what we were talking about, Folly?' he asked as she turned away from her new acquaintance and walked with Roland to the settee on the other side of the room.

'No. You were saying you loved me, and showing me how much when the call-boy interrupted you. You seem to have changed your mind though, for you don't look as if you love me now, and you haven't said two words to me since I came into the room.'

'That was not my fault. You have given half your time to that fool, Delaunay's friend.'

'*That* fool spoke to me when he wanted to,' answered Folly, tartly.

'I dare say I am unreasonable and all that, but it irritates me to see you exposed to the impudence of every puppy that comes into this room. I wish I could take you away from this sort of life.'

'Away from the stage?' asked Folly, opening her eyes wide. 'I thought you said you loved me.'

'So I do, Folly!'

'And don't you know that I could never be happy away from the stage?'

'Would the life of an ordinary lady be insupportable to you?'

'Yes. What position could equal mine here? What girl is there that people crowd to see? that has her name written up in beautiful big letters everywhere? whose portrait is in all the windows for people to admire? who has bouquets thrown at her feet every night? who's applauded when she dances, or sings, or even stands still? who has poetry written about her, and is talked of in the newspapers more than the queen herself? Why, to give up all that and live mewed up in a house, seeing half-a-dozen people a week, would be like going back to service and drudgery.'

'But is this life not deficient in something which you might find in retirement? Could nothing compensate you for the loss of flattery and the homage of idle sight-seers?'

'Nothing—nothing on earth—except—' Folly paused, wondering if she could resign flattery even to restore her father to health and happiness.

'Excepting what, Folly?'

'Never mind—nothing that you can offer. Come,' she said, changing her attitude as if to get away from the painful image of her father which had come before her mind—'Come, you had good news to tell me, and I have heard nothing.'

'Is it nothing to know that I love you?'

'That is no news. You have loved me a long time—ever since you first saw me.'

'I think you are right, Folly; I must have loved you at first sight, though I dared not admit it even to myself. I could not love you conscientiously while I was engaged to Miss Vane.'

'Conscientiously—what's that?'

'With justice to my own conscience—my sense of right and wrong.'

'And now you can?'

'Yes; I am no longer under any engagement.'

'I see. So now you can love me conscientiously. Read me your father's letter. Does he know that you love me?'

'Yes. He knows more than I thought he knew. Vane must have told him. It was he, you know, who looked after me when you brought me home from that precious ball.'

'Why did he tell your father?'

'He wanted my father to recall me from London, I dare say.'

'Ah, he didn't want his sister to lose you.'

'No, that was not his reason. Vane would do nothing mean like that. He is the most generous, unselfish man living.'

Roland spoke with his old warmth.

'Then what was his reason?'

'I think he was afraid I should get into trouble, or—or go wrong in some way,' Roland replied, stammering, and pulling his slight moustache.

'He was afraid of me?'

'Perhaps so.'

'And your father is afraid of his sister?'

'Well, possibly,' Roland assented.

Folly began to see things more clearly.

'Your father approves of your loving me conscientiously?' she said, emphasising the long word which seemed agreeable to her.

'He puts no restrictions on me, and he gives me permission to draw upon him for more money if I require it. That is the good news I wanted to tell you.'

But somehow he did not feel as if he were telling good news, and she expressed no pleasure in hearing it. She seemed to be occupied with some mental analysis, for after a minute's silence she said:

'Loving conscientiously—I don't quite understand that word yet awhile. When you loved Miss Vane conscientiously what did you mean?'

'That I would be true to her; and that's what I mean by loving you conscientiously.'

Roland flattered himself he was getting out of the difficulty now.

'And by being true to her you intended to marry her; is that what you mean by loving me conscientiously?'

Roland looked down in silent embarrassment.

'There never was such an unlucky beggar as I am when I open my mouth,' thought he; 'I am sure to use some word that can be twisted up into a lash for my own shoulders.'

'That is what you mean, Roland?' continued Folly, speaking with unwonted quickness and excitement. 'And your father sends you money that you may marry me—is it so?'

Roland twisted his fingers, keeping his eyes on the ground and blushing with honest shame.

'Sir Andrew thinks it will be more to your honour when you are a justice of the peace and a Member of Parliament to have a wife like me, the daughter of a—' she checked herself, and, avoiding the word, said, 'Better to have a wife who was born in a workhouse than the simple sister of a good man—is it so?'

'I will not lie, Folly,' said Roland, lifting up his head. 'It is not so. My father would rather see me dead than married to you!'

'Have you any more good news to tell

A Proposal.   167

me?' Folly asked, with a short forced laugh.

He bowed his head again.

Folly's face was white with anger. At one moment she turned her hand upon her lap to strike him across the face with her knuckles before everyone in that room.

He had offered her the insult she most dreaded. He had thought her capable of descending to the level of common girls. He had wronged her as much as it was in his power to wrong her.

With an effort she overcame the impulse as the old idea of a deep and thorough vengeance presented itself again to her mind.

'I am afraid I have been fool enough to say more than I should,' said Roland, noticing her silence, feeling that it must be all over between them now; 'but I hope that despite this misunderstanding——'

'There is no misunderstanding,' replied Folly, 'but there might have been had you concealed anything. I see all without any mistake whatever. I can see your father just as I see you, and the Margaret you have left, and her brother who would take you away from me—I see you, every one, quite clearly.'

The second act was called, and a general movement took place, in which Folly joined.

'You will suffer me to wait for you?' said Roland.

Folly nodded and left the room with the rest.

At the close of the second act, instead of returning to the green-room, Folly retired to her dressing-room.

She sent her dresser away, and locked herself in. Then she sat down and brooded over what had transpired between herself and Roland. There were new proofs to convince her of Sir Andrew's heartless indifference to any interests outside his own. She saw him with his ugly faults distorted into hideous vices. She was merciless in her judgment of Roland. Prejudice blinded her to all that might excuse him. His very virtues she construed into subtle artifices employed to weaken her defence and cheat her reason. Father and son were alike— they had done all in their power to degrade her father and herself.

She knew nothing of religion beyond what she had seen upon the stage and through the doors of churches. She understood that there was a God who deals punishment to the wicked, who taught that law of vengeance she had learnt by heart, and she knew that He was to be moved by prayer.

She rose suddenly from her seat, and dropping upon her knees said through her closed teeth :

'Give me vengeance, great God, and let me punish these men as they deserve.'

CHAPTER XI.

VANE IS INTRODUCED TO FOLLY.

ROLAND had tried so long and persistently to cheat himself into the belief that wrong is right, that he found it difficult now clearly to distinguish one from the other. He was mystified and perplexed between the true and the false views he had taken of his connection with Folly. This mental disorder was increased by the physical results of late hours, want of rest, and a vicious use of stimulants.

He did not distinctly see what he was doing, or what he must do as the inevitable consequence of what he had done. In this deplorable state of obscurity—a state which distinguishes the earlier stages of insanity—

he abandoned himself to the chance guidance of circumstances, like a man adrift on the bare sea who has neither chart nor compass to appeal to.

He felt that he had 'got into another mess,' of a rather more desperate kind than any he had yet got out of; and could only hope that 'the luck' which had assisted him in previous difficulties would not desert him now, but would ultimately shape his rough-hewed ends satisfactorily.

It must be owned that he was uneasy as to the future, and looked for the first time doubtfully at 'the luck.' Before, he had felt that his good intentions and general honesty of principle entitled him to the favours of Fortune; but now he had no feeling of this kind to encourage his hope. He was conscious of being debased from his honest manhood, of having gone quite astray from the path of rectitude, which, despite his frequent deviations in former times, he had never lost sight of.

Moreover, he missed the trusty friend who had never failed him in critical moments; who had forgiven him, and lifted him out of the mire, and sent him before the world again clean and respectable, no matter how he had transgressed. Richard Vane was no longer his friend; he had done that which the patient vicar could not forgive; he dreaded the possibility of accidentally meeting him, and found satisfaction in the thought that the breach he had made was wide enough to keep them asunder.

He was wretched enough as he sat in the green-room waiting for Folly. When she did not come at the conclusion of the second act, he perceived that he had offended her for whom he had forsaken all.

'I haven't a friend in the world, and I suppose I don't deserve one,' he said to himself, bitterly.

At that very moment the commissionaire from the stage-door entered the room, and, handing a card to Roland, said:

'The gentleman's waiting outside, sir.'

Upon the card was written 'Richard Vane,' in the vicar's well-known hand.

The blood rushed to Roland's face, and he felt as he remembered feeling when a boy, caught by this same gentle friend—then his usher—caught dropping over the orchard wall with full pockets.

'Shall I ask him to walk in, sir?' asked the

messenger, recalling Roland to his present position.

'Eh? Yes—yes; that is, no; I will come out,' answered Roland, in some confusion; then, suddenly remembering that Folly might come to the room the next moment expecting to find him, he recalled the commissionaire and said he had changed his mind, and would see Mr. Vane there. With this order the man retired.

Roland tried in vain to settle on some definite plan of action, but he had not decided whether to receive Richard Vane with formal politeness or the warmth of an old friend, when the commissionaire returned followed by the gaunt vicar. Roland's colour left him, and his fingers, resting on the table, trembled —not from vermouth this time, but from the emotion he felt in looking in the plain face of the high-shouldered vicar.

He did not see the red nose and the yellow skin that attracted the critical notice of the two or three other spectators; he saw only the soft, sweet eyes that rested tenderly on himself, which were lit with something of that divine love which passeth all understanding.

Vane took his hand, and, holding it still, said:

'Your hand's not right, Roley, and your face is as pale as a muffin. What's the matter with you?'

'Nothing,' answered Roland, falteringly; 'it's the vermouth, perhaps. Who'd have expected to see you here?'

'It is a rather uncanonical place for a parson; but it is a place I wished to see, nevertheless. As a boy I remember to have had a passionate longing to see the inside of a Punch-and-Judy show.'

'There isn't much in it, after all, is there?' said Roland, looking round the room and gaining confidence.

The vicar noticed that the fingers ceased to tremble.

'Thank heaven it isn't vermouth!' he said to himself, allowing the hand to slip from his.

'I can't offer to show you the other parts of the stage just now; it is against the regulations during the performance.'

'There is one part of the stage which one may see without infringing the rules, I expect. Is there a seat to be had? I want to see Folly.'

'Do you! Come along with me; I have a box. Quick! the orchestra is rung in, and we shall just be in time for Folly's great scene.' Roland spoke with excitement. He was anxious that Richard Vane should see Folly in all her beauty, that he might be forgiven for loving her so madly.

His enthusiasm was not unnoticed. Vane reverenced earnestness, and so that Roland loved Folly thoroughly all might be well. What he loathed and dreaded to find his friend indulging in was trifling and vermouth.

The curtain was rising as the two gentlemen came to the front of the box.

'Take my glass,' whispered Roland eagerly, thrusting a lorgnette forward. Vane pushed it away gently, without taking his eyes from the tableau before him.

Folly as Andromeda chained to the rock was to Richard Vane's eyes the most beautiful picture he had ever looked upon. He was no green novice; he had seen scores of Andromedas in the picture-galleries of Europe, and he had seen dozens of burlesques. What he saw gained much of its charm, perhaps, from the contrast it afforded to what he had expected to see. In a burlesque of Andromeda it was reasonable to suppose that the chained heroine would appear in French boots and in a dress as much like an acrobat's as possible; that she would wear a simper on her face, and jewellery of an equally false character upon her fingers; and that the *tout ensemble* would be to the last degree vulgar. Folly's Andromeda was as simple an appeal to the sense of beauty which all possess as a Greek marble. A soft, diaphanous fabric veiled her figure from the shoulder to the foot, falling in graceful folds that yielded to the contour of her body and limbs. The diamonds she displayed in the preceding acts she abandoned in this; hands, arms, and throat were bare. The rich clusters of her hair drawn away from one cheek hung tumbled and loose upon the other, as if the creeping sea-breeze had blown them there. There was no straining after effect either in her pose or in the expression of her face. The picture was composed by Art, and painted by Nature, in bold defiance to all the laws of burlesque. The conception was Folly's own, which had been reluctantly accepted by the manager as a hazardous experiment, with that fortunate result which attended every innovation made upon the stage by the girl. The manager attributed these innovations to caprice; but they were undoubtedly the emanations of genius, absurd as it may seem to attribute the divine creative faculty to the actor of anything lower than tragedy.

Richard looked on in silent emotion—the emotion that a delicate mind experiences in the presence of a sunrise, of twilight, of a melody, of anything which is essentially lovely. But apart from this sense his heart was touched with a pathetic interest in the young girl upon the stage, which perhaps no one in the house but he felt.

Roland watched the expression of sympathy and delight grow in his companion's face with trembling pleasure.

'Now, thought he, he must know why I cannot tear myself from London; he must envy me the love of such an angel.'

He would not by a movement venture to break Richard Vane's rapture until the delight of the audience rising from a murmur found expression in loud applause. Then he faced to the stage, and, fixing his ardent eyes upon his darling, clapped his hands as vigorously as any pit admirer.

He turned round to see why Vane did not join in the applause. The vicar's hands were idle on his knee. He had taken his eyes from the stage and was regarding the rows of spectators that filled the house from stalls to gallery, each one noisily expressing his appreciation; from these he looked to the young girl who, flushed with pleasure, was acknowledging the ovation; and then he said gently:

'Poor child!'

He did not again take his eyes from Folly while she remained upon the scene. When she withdrew he leaned back in his seat and spoke to Roland.

'I want you to introduce me to Folly,' he said.

'With the greatest pleasure,' Roland answered, still anxious that Vane should admire her. Immediately after he reflected that Folly might appear less charming off the stage, especially if the captious humour she had displayed in the early part of the evening continued, and he repented making the promise so hastily.

'Shall you see her before we go home?'

'Yes; this act is the last,' Roland replied. Then he thought, 'What the deuce can Dick have to say to her?'

'By-the-bye, I have not mentioned yet that I purpose being your guest to-night. You can give me a shake-down, I dare say.'

'Of course I can.' And then Roland wondered how he was to square this arrangement with his usual attention to Folly.

At that moment Folly ran on to the stage in another costume and presented another side of her character to Richard Vane. Her gaiety was so spontaneous and natural, so entirely free from vulgarity, that it charmed the vicar completely. He had been prepared to find her a girl above the ordinary kind, nevertheless her strikingly exceptional character astonished him.

When the curtain fell, they went down by a private staircase to the stage, and Roland showed his friend what was to be seen while they waited for Folly to come down from her dressing-room.

The scenery was removed, the curtain rolled up, the front of the house in gloom, and only a few gaslights casting a dim light over the dusty stage when Folly came down wrapped in her furs and approached the two gentlemen.

She had seen Richard Vane in the box, and guessed that he came to remove Roland from her power.

She turned brusquely away as soon as the formal ceremony of the introduction was over, and, going away a few steps, called Roland to her side.

'What does he want?' she asked.

'To be introduced to you.'

'Well, he has been introduced. What is he waiting for?'

'You see, he has asked himself to go home with me, and I can't exactly say he can't,' Roland replied, nervously.

'Why not?'

'He's my friend, you know.'

'And what am I?' she asked, dropping her voice to its softest tones, and looking into his eyes with a maddening little smile.

'Folly!—Love! Bid me do what you will, and it shall be done. But think what I owe my friend.'

Richard Vane stood where he had been left in the centre of the stage. As Roland spoke Folly moved slowly away, widening the distance. 'I will show you what to do,' she said, a ludicrous spirit of mischief rising over her more serious feelings.

They reached the wings, walking in the slow manner of those engaged in conversation, then she hastened her steps, taking his arm, and said :

'Lead me to my brougham.'

He led her to the carriage waiting for her, put her in, and held out his hand to bid her good-night. Holding his hand, she said:
'Come in.'
'But Vane——'
'Come in,' she repeated, in a voice more tenderly sweet.

Without further hesitation he stepped into the brougham.

'Now tell the man to drive to the supper-rooms.'

'But Dick, there—all alone.'

'Would you leave me all alone?' she asked, in pitiful accents.

Roland put his head out of window, and shouted to the driver.

The next moment the brougham was rattling away from the theatre over the uneven stones of the back street.

Richard Vane waited patiently on the stage until the stage-manager came and asked him whom he was waiting for.

'Mr. Aveling,' said the vicar.

'Why, he's been gone this half-hour. Went with Folly. I heard him tell the driver to go to the Hyperion Supper-Rooms myself,' answered the stage-manager.

'Thank you. Will you show me the way

out?' Vane said quietly, without expressing surprise.

He was led to the street, when he walked calmly to Roland's chambers in Kensington, and there waited for his host, reading the neglected Buckle like a sensible man.

CHAPTER XII.

A KISS.

FOLLY did not give Roland time to think of repentance. Over supper she made him drink 'to absent friends,' and join her in laughing at the practical joke played upon Mr. Vane. This was another of those scrapes which he would have to get out of 'somehow.' How could he think of unpleasant consequences or be dull with Folly doing her utmost to charm and bewilder him?

When they left the Hyperion, Folly proposed having a drive—the mist of yesterday had given place to a clear frosty air—and he accepted, as indeed he would have done under any circumstances, being excited with light wine and bright glances from the most beautiful of eyes.

They were driven along Regent Street and Oxford Street until they reached the Marble Arch; then the brougham was turned homewards. At the bottom of Park Lane Folly said she would like to walk home through the Park, so they left the brougham.

'You don't want to go home and be lectured by that ugly old fellow, do you?' asked Folly, turning Roland towards Buckingham Palace.

'I never want to leave you, Folly. I wonder what old Dick wanted to say to you?'

'He wanted to preach a long sermon on the sinfulness of taking you away from his sister, I dare say. That would make no difference to me, would it to you?'

'No argument in the world could make me love you less.'

'You are a good boy.'

'I wasn't at the beginning of the evening, Folly.'

'Oh, you must forget that. I was out of temper about something. Those new shoes of mine don't fit, and you know how irritable I am. I am not ill-tempered now.'

'You are a darling, Folly.'

'I dare say I was a little jealous of that man's sister, and annoyed because you couldn't marry me. But you love me all the same.'

'I don't think any man on earth loves as I love you.'

'Of course you couldn't marry a girl who is only an actress.'

'These abominable social restrictions are the only impediment. Still I don't see the enormous importance of marriage. A man can love without marrying.'

Roland spoke in perfect innocence, and contemplated a platonic affection as quite possible; but Folly, who had no sentiment in the affair, saw it merely from a common-sense point of view.

She did not answer. Despite her desire to hold Roland in her power, she could not even verbally acquiesce in a proposition which her very soul revolted against.

'However, Folly,' pursued Roland, 'we need talk no more upon that subject. We will go on just the same as ever, you know, and let things settle down into their proper places as circumstances direct. This letter of the governor's comes just in the right time, for my funds are as low as they can get comfortably; and now I can furnish a little house for you, and get you away from that murky hole in Lambeth?'

'Yes, yes, that will be nice. When shall we look for a house?'

'Directly. Oh, it will be famous fun. I should like a little place with a stable, so that you could have a pair of ponies and a pony carriage.'

'And drive them myself to the theatre and back again?'

'Yes, when the weather is good. A nice comfortable little affair, with just room for you and me, darling, in the front, and a seat behind for a buttoney boy.'

'Oh!' Folly exclaimed, with her old childish delight.

Then she forgot all about the ugly side of the picture, and dwelt long on the charming prospect opened to her; proposing and arranging a thousand particulars in a gay, light-hearted, open spirit, until they came to the end of the Lambeth Road, and she suddenly remembered her father; then her bright fancies vanished at once, like a broken bubble, and left her with the dismal reflection that her happiness was only one of those things which might have been.

Roland knew nothing of the dull despondency that had suddenly succeeded to Folly's gay hopefulness. Her last laugh still rippled in his ear; her silence and her sigh he misunderstood.

'We will part here,' she said, stopping.

He made arrangements for meeting her in the afternoon, to which she responded in monosyllables, and then held out her hand, saying: 'And now good-night.'

The warmth had not diminished in Roland's heart; he took her sudden silence as significant of regret at parting; he was emboldened by his own fancies.

'Folly,' he said, holding her hand closely, 'I have never kissed you. May I to-night?'

She bent her head, and a shudder ran through her. Then she thought of her father, and, closing her eyes, she held up her cheek.

Roland touched the smooth surface lightly with his lips, and left her with a fever in his veins.

A fever of another kind quickened Folly's pulses. When she had gone a dozen steps alone she stooped down quickly to a puddle in the road, dipped her handkerchief in the water and rubbed her cheek with it where Roland's lips had touched.

* * * * *

It was a quarter past two when Roland reached Grandison Chambers and walked upstairs to his apartments, wondering how he should excuse his conduct to Richard Vane. He did not dread the meeting now; his love of Folly and the hope that she was beginning to love him made him reckless. He felt very little more than the disinclination to anything like a 'scene' which is common to people of soft indolent dispositions.

He opened the door gently, hoping that Vane might have turned into bed. He had seen a light in the room from without, and knew by that he had a visitor. He found the vicar wide awake; Buckle did not send him to sleep.

'Are you very angry with me, Dick?' he asked, as he faced his old friend.

'Not yet. I am in the neutral position of one who doesn't know whether he should be angry or not,' answered Vane, slipping an envelope in the page and closing his book. 'Tell me why you left me in that odd manner, and you will soon see what the condition of my temper is.'

'You may be sure I didn't wish to offend you; but it is rather hard to explain why I treated you so rudely.'

'If you tell me it was unavoidable I shall be content.'

'Of course I could have returned to you if I liked, in fact I did try——'

Roland hesitated, wishing Vane to think ill of him rather than of Folly, but not seeing how to exonerate her and inculpate himself.

Richard saw pretty clearly how it was with him.

'You were divided between duty to your friend and your love to Folly, eh?'

'Yes, and I decided for Folly,' Roland said, boldly.

'You would not have loved her sincerely had you not, and insincerity to her is what I could not forgive in you.'

With eager enthusiasm Roland answered:

'Oh, Dick, I do love her with all my heart and soul! What else could reconcile me to alienation from my friends?'

CHAPTER XIII.

FATHER AND DAUGHTER.

ROLAND'S spirits rose. Everything was going well with him now. Even Dick, whom he most feared, was kind and seemed to approve of his loving Folly. It surprised him to think that such a change should take place in so short a space of time; and he wondered how it was he had looked at the affair in such a gloomy and despondent spirit.

'Let us sit down and have a good talk,' he said, pushing forward a chair.

'No, thank you,' replied Vane, as he looked at his watch. 'Half-past two is too early for me. We will talk later in the day.'

'Oh, don't turn in yet awhile. Have something to drink. Do you like *mousseux?*'

'Very much. But my condition is suggestive of a sleepier wine.'

' A half bottle,' urged Roland, feeling that it would be impossible to sleep yet awhile.

' No, I don't want it, and you don't need it. Come, where shall I sleep ?'

Finding it impossible to move Vane from his purpose, Roland made the necessary arrangements for his visitor, and afterwards prepared himself for rest, unusual as the hour was for his repose.

In half an hour Vane was sound asleep. Roland sat irresolute on the side of his bed.

' What on earth is the good of putting out the light yet ? I can't go to sleep,' thought he. ' I wish we had opened a bottle. I must try and read myself to sleep.'

He turned the gas up, and made the experiment with a book. In five minutes he laid the novel aside with the conviction that it is not a wise thing to read when one's dry. He stared at the gas and thought of Folly until his ideas got confused and his eyes felt heavy. If the gas were lower he thought he could go to sleep now. He turned it down, and getting into bed again tried to sleep.

' I never can sleep on my right side,' said he, turning over after a couple of minutes;

but the left was equally uncomfortable, so he lay on his back, and soon after began to gasp like a fish out of water. 'If Vane had not "notions" about drinking in the night I would have half a bottle now,' thought he. Presently he sat up in bed and entertained serious thoughts of drinking a tumbler of water. 'It's about the worst thing a man can drink, the doctors agree upon that point; but this thirst is intolerable. Now, if Vane weren't asleep I'd have a *demi;* but it would be a shame to wake him, and he'd lecture for an hour. If I could only go to sleep——' He threw himself back on the pillow and shut his eyes savagely.

'Are you asleep, Vane?' he cried out, about two minutes later. There was no answer. That settled the business. Roland sprang out of bed, turned up the gas, got one of his favourites from the cupboard, took off its straw cap, and removed the wires with an amount of celerity that bespoke a willing mind. The skill with which he got the cork out without allowing it to wake the sleeper in the next apartment was commendable, and so adroitly was the feat executed that not a single drop of the frothy liquid was wasted.

'I knew it would revive me,' said he, finishing the bottle. 'It always does.'

He was quite right, it did revive him. He was less inclined to sleep than ever. However, now that his thirst was allayed he could lie and think dreamily of Folly without discomfort. It was not until four o'clock that this indeterminate condition became irksome; but at five it was unendurable. He could not think consistently upon any subject for two minutes together, and he could not avoid trying to think consistently.

'It's as bad as being mad, to lie and rave in one's thoughts like this; I must do something to go to sleep,' said he, throwing the clothes off. They felt like bonds upon him.

'Doing something' meant drinking some poisonous liquor from a bottle which he took from a drawer. Whether he took more or less than his customary dose of the oily green syrup he did not know or care in his drowsy, half-idiotic state. It acted as a narcotic, and sent him off to sleep with a delicious vision of Folly's pretty face.

He slept like a bear until Richard Vane shook him into wakefulness at half-past nine.

'H'loa, old man; that you? Where am

I?' What is it?' he asked, trying to open his eyes.

'Where does Folly live?' Vane asked in return.

'Folly? Lambeth Road. Wait a bit, I shall be awake directly.'

'What number in Lambeth Road?'

'Twenty-seven. But what's matter? Nothing happened?'

"Nothing. Go to sleep again.'

'Thanks; have breakfast, you know—make 'self at home—all right,' the last words ended in a deep sigh, and were immediately succeeded by a snore.

Vane had already made himself at home and eaten his breakfast, and now, having the information he required, he left Kensington and walked by Victoria Station and Horseferry Road into Lambeth.

The houses in Lambeth Road were being renumbered—some had the new numbers, others retained the old, and a large portion of them showed impartiality by having no numbers at all.

Vane, after some trouble, found out which way the new numbers ran, and had traced them from 150 down to 41, when his attention was attracted by a little knot of people gathered before a house some distance in advance of him. A turfed forecourt lay between the house and the pavement; from the outer side the spectators commanded a view of the whole front of the house—a gratifying privilege to the morbid.

It was generally understood that a woman was being murdered within, and, as is usual in such cases, every one was deeply interested, but not one moved a hand to avert the mischief. A woman from the adjoining house had come down to look up at the windows, and was talking in a low deprecatory tone, to which the crowd lent their ears without removing their eyes from the house.

'He oughtn't to be kep' in the house with them two females. I see him the other day with a knife in his hand,' the woman was saying as Vane came up.

He looked at the door, saw upon it the number he sought, and without a moment's hesitation pushed his way through the idlers, ran across the forecourt and thundered at the door.

'It ain't no good your knocking, young man; Miss Clip is out, and the old man's killin' the other female,' said the neighbour.

Vane waited a second, then knocked again.

'I tell you it ain't no good,' the woman repeated.

Vane put his ear to the door, and then, stepping back a pace, turned his shoulder to the door and threw the whole weight of his body against the lock. The door, secured only by the latch, flew open, and Vane entered. The crowd, excited to greater curiosity, impinged on the forecourt and showed a desire now of following his lead. He closed the door, shot a bolt, and paused, listening.

'Let me go, or I'll do for you!' squeaked a thin, reedy voice, that seemed to come from a room below.

Vane found the stairs, and ran down. Opening a door and entering a stone-paved scullery, a strange sight met his eyes—an old man struggling with a young girl.

The girl was Folly.

The old man stood against the whitened walls—a gaunt, large-framed man, shrunk away, wasted, distorted with disease, privations, and years of misery, dressed in gentlemanly clothes and white linen.

He was pinned against the wall by the wrists; his wristbands were smeared with blood; it was his, and yet not his—drops fell upon the stone pavement from the hand of the daughter, who stayed him from doing a greater harm. His face was purple with excitement; his thin white hair, tumbled and disordered, fell over his protruding, bloodshot eyes; his nostrils were dilated; his mouth gaped open; the turgid veins stood out from his face and skinny throat. He looked like what he was—a maniac. In his right hand he grasped a carving-knife with a horn handle.

In physical strength the girl had the advantage; nevertheless, it was evident that her hold upon the old man was relaxing. Upon her face was a look of distressed compassion. Her power to control her antagonist diminished as she perceived how it exasperated him to greater fury. As her resolution gave way, as she yielded to the tender feeling of compassion, the old man's nervous force increased, his determination growing with his ascendancy over her. He clutched his claw-like fingers with a tighter hold upon the buckhorn-handled knife. He writhed and struggled to free his wrists from her grasp, snapping at her arms with his toothless gums, and kicking her savagely. Happily the shoes upon his feet were of felt, nevertheless she suffered.

'Oh! father, father! you are hurting me,' she said, in a tone of gentle remonstrance.

He laughed, with a horrible sound, the foam falling from his mouth upon the scattered grey hairs of his beard, and kicked with redoubled violence.

The noise made by the old man prevented his hearing Vane's approach. As the door opened, and he saw him, he ceased to struggle. Recognising at once that here was one not to be subdued, he dropped the knife from his hand, and sank upon his knees in abject trepidation.

'I didn't mean to hurt her,' he whimpered. 'I was only going to cut a piece of bread, that's all. She began it, not me; she was trying to kill me. I never did anything to hurt anyone. I am only a poor old man. She is the strong one; look at my arms and look at hers. *What* chance have I against her? That's my blood on her hand—oh dear! oh dear!' With transparent cunning he whipped a handkerchief from his pocket and bound it about his scathless hand. 'She is always trying to kill me, trying to get me into trouble. I don't want the knife—I don't want anything—except to live quietly, like a poor old man. Don't hurt me—don't set things to hunt me about—not, you know, dead hares; let me die nice and quietly. It's all this girl, not me—she wants to get rid of me, she does.'

He spoke with his head on Folly's bosom, for the girl had thrown herself down beside him and drawn his head to her heart.

'You mustn't believe her. She does this to deceive you,' he continued. 'She would have cut my throat if you had not come in at that moment to save the poor old man.'

'There, there, dear; you're quite safe now,' murmured Folly, stroking back his hair and smoothing it over his head.

'Your hand is hurt; let me see it,' said Richard Vane to Folly.

'No, it is nothing,' said she, snatching it away. 'I scratched it.'

'Yes, yes, she scratched it, I saw her,' piped John Morrison. 'Poor Folly—I'll see to it.'

But Vane was not to be put away; he took Folly's hand forcibly, and found two of the fingers cut on the inner side, where she had apparently clasped the knife to take it from her father. He would sicken if he saw a crushed dog, but he was not squeamish at the sight of blood when his help was needed.

He looked at Folly's wound. The cuts were not deep. Vane tore his handkerchief in half and bound up the fingers with a firm yet tender hand, that showed him used to rendering practical assistance.

The old man, exhausted by his late exertions, and no longer stimulated by hopes of supremacy, could hardly support himself upon his knees, yet his fear of Richard Vane prevented his relaxing into that state of prostration which usually followed violent paroxysms of this kind. He cowered now for protection beside the daughter whom but for Vane he would have murdered; and she, keeping her left arm about his neck, showed far more concern for him than for herself. After yielding to have her wounded fingers dressed, she seemed to forget the man who had probably saved her life.

John Morrison, seeing that nothing was to be gained by vilifying Folly, tried to ingratiate himself in Vane's favour by other means.

'Poor, dear Folly!' he said in a cracked, whining voice, intended to imply affectionate sympathy, vigilantly watching Vane's face as he spoke. 'Dear, dear Folly! scratched her hand, so she did; she said so. She never tells lies, never says there isn't any rum when I know there is. Scratched her hands, so she did, and the kind, strong gentleman is tying them up for her. The good, strong gentleman who wouldn't set the—the dead things to hunt me even if I did lose my temper for once in a way. He wouldn't set dead little babies, and hares with great, long, stiff backs and stiff legs, to chase me about, because he knows I love my dear Folly, and always do as she asks me, except one little time when I lost my temper just a tiny minute because she wouldn't give me money to go out and buy her a little present—yes, buy her a little present; that's what I wanted the money for—it wasn't rum for myself, but a little present for her. Yes, that was it. No one ever tells lies now. So the good, strong gentleman will be kind to me, won't he, and forget anything he might have thought he saw?'

'Yes, the strong gentleman is very sorry for you,' said Vane, kindly.

'*You* are not telling lies, are you? You wouldn't say you're very sorry for me and then go and set dead things and little babies——'

'Father, father, you shall always be safe

with me,' cried the girl, clasping the hand which Vane had just released with the other about her father's neck. 'You shall never be persecuted any more if you will only trust to me, and do as I ask you.'

'Yes, dear little babies,' continued the old man, seeing the advantage he had won. 'And your mother—dead too. So pretty; like you, Folly, with the mole on her cheek there where yours is.'

John Morrison had used his tenderest memories as instruments to work upon the feelings of his daughter, until they continued no longer to touch his own heart. It was with them just as it is with the frequent repetition of a tender word, which ceases in time to carry with it the import of its earlier utterance.

To Folly this callousness was more touching than his first passionate reference to her dead mother. It was dreadful that he should suffer, but still more painful to think he could not suffer. Looking at him she could only think of the higher humanity from which he had sunk to this almost brutal indifference. She seemed to see him with a living body and a dead soul.

With a passionate cry of grief she buried

her face in his shoulder, as if to avoid the sight which met her eyes, and burst into tears.

'Lookey, lookey,' said the old man, laying his face against the girl's beautiful head, but keeping his eyes craftily upon Richard; 'lookey; see; if I *did* lose my temper just for a moment, I wasn't to blame. She is sorry for what she has done and cries for pardon, and I forgive her; and so you won't set any—things, you know what, to hunt me, will you?'

Richard Vane shook his head, and stood looking at Folly for a minute in silence—unable to take his eyes from the pathetic picture of filial devotion—then he picked up the knife from the ground and noiselessly left the room.

He believed that the old man was powerless to attack the girl, but he paused outside the door to find what use John Morrison would make of his absence.

'He's gone, Folly; the strong man has gone,' said the old man in a whistling whisper; 'but I'll not be angry again if you'll give me only a little tiny drop of rum.'

'You cannot have it until the doctor comes. Rest still; it is not long to wait, dear.'

Folly spoke in the soothing tone of a mother to her fractious child.

'Well, I'll be still if you'll promise to protect me if the strong man returns.'

There was a quick knock at the street-door, and Vane, satisfied that no further mischief was to be apprehended immediately from the old man, left the basement and opened the street-door.

The crowd still gaped over the railings of the forecourt; a pale and excited woman stood on the doorstep.

'What's the matter, sir? My name's Miss Clip. I live here,' she said, entering the hall. 'What has happened to Miss Folly?'

'Nothing very serious,' answered Vane, closing the door.

'Oh dear, they said outside she was murdered, and, indeed, I shouldn't be surprised if she was. I can't always be with her; and he's so cunning there's no knowing what he's after. He seemed to be sound asleep when I went out a quarter of an hour ago. It isn't safe for a young girl, with a merciful, tender heart like hers, to be in the power of an old madman. But there, she won't let anyone else take charge of him when she can; and as for sending him away, she'd never forgive you for proposing of it.'

The little woman would have said much more, for she was one of those creatures who cannot be silent when they have the chance of being heard, but Vane checked her.

'I think you may be of assistance now; go down and see. I will wait here a few minutes, in case I may be wanted.'

Miss Clip ran away, removing her bonnet and cloak as she went; in a few minutes she returned.

'Miss Folly begs me to give her compliments, and say she's much obliged to you for calling and being so kind, but she feels quite safe now, and won't trouble you to wait any longer.'

No one knowing Folly could have believed this message to be hers; it was, indeed, a euphemism of Miss Clip's own concoction, as Richard Vane knew perfectly well, for Folly's words, spoken in clear, unmistakable tones, had come to his ears from below. These were the words he had heard: 'I know the man quite well, Clip. He's the parson who wants Roland Aveling to marry his sister, and thinks he'll get him away from me. Tell him I don't want to know more of him than I know at present. I never want to see him again, and I don't thank him for coming without an invitation. Don't answer, Clip. Isn't it enough for me to see my father's degradation? Have I any reason to be grateful for having it published to all the world? Tell him what I say. Go.'

CHAPTER XIV.

ANOTHER LECTURE.

WHEN Richard Vane returned to Grandison Chambers he found Roland up and dressed.

'Holloa, Vane, where the deuce have you been?' were the young man's first words.

Vane did not reply to the question. He looked into Roland's face with stern scrutinising eyes as he took the offered hand, and compared him with Folly. Roland could not meet his friend's glance. There was a wavering, shifty, shameful look in the young fellow's dull eyes and pale face. His hand was unwholesomely damp and cold. Despite the good spirits in which he had gone to bed, he had risen with his customary feeling of dejection and infirmity. He was now painfully conscious of his feebleness, and wanted something to conceal his feelings, and, as he took his hand from Vane's and sought the toothpick in his waistcoat pocket, his fingers trembled so that he could not readily get at it. Knowing that Vane's eyes observed his futility, he removed his hand with an impatient exclamation, and thrust it in the wide pocket of his morning jacket.

'What is the matter with you this morning?' asked Vane.

'Out of sorts. Couldn't get to sleep. Went to bed too early.'

'Nonsense. Going to bed early does not make a man's hand shake like that in the morning. What did you drink before you went to sleep?'

'A little *mousseux*.'

'I saw the bottle; that wouldn't account for it.'

Vane crossed to the cupboard where Roland kept his wines, and used his eyes.

'What in the name of all that's horrible are these?' he asked, taking out first one and then another of the precious patent drugs.

'You see what they are,' Roland answered,

pettishly. He didn't like the tone in which Vane read the hybrid Greek and Latin names on the pet nostrums, nor the sarcastic voice in which he read aloud the advertised efficacy of the doses. It was a freedom which even friendship could not justify.

'Ugh!' grunted the vicar, pushing them aside and looking in the corners.

'I hope your curiosity is satisfied, Dick?'

'Not quite. I am looking for the other poison.'

'What other poison?' Roland knew perfectly well what was meant.

Vane turned sharply round, and with angry contempt said:

'Are you not ashamed to play at lying, Roland? Sit down there and listen to me. I find I must treat you like a child. Sit down, or your feeble legs will give way under you; sit down this minute.'

Roland made a faint show of opposition, and then sat down.

'What I mean is this, you have been drugging yourself with something worse than the stuff quack doctors invent: absinthe or vermouth, or some vile poison of that kind. Where is it?'

'In the drawer of the *armoire* in the next room.'

Vane went to the receptacle and fished out the bottle. Through the opened window he flung it out on to the tiles of the adjoining outbuildings.

'Do you know how long a man has to live who takes to drugging his body with vermouth?' he asked, coming back to the sitting-room.

Roland did not reply.

'About seven years; his reason goes in about six.' Vane continued, 'Now what do you think of the man who escapes his obligations to society by cutting his throat?'

'I think he is a coward.'

'So do I. But he takes a less cowardly means of doing a cowardly thing than you would.'

'Why do you take such trouble about me? If I'm going to the devil, why don't you let me go my own way?'

'You won't excite my sympathy by that *ad misericordiam* style of argument. You are humbugging yourself, not me.'

'I don't ask for your sympathy; I only ask you to let me alone.'

'I should not do that, if you only were to

be considered; I certainly shall not, having the interests of some one else at heart.'

'I do not see who else is concerned.'

Roland ventured to raise his eyes to Vane, who had taken a seat facing him, and cowered before the angry look which gave him the lie. He saw that his companion was not to be trifled with, and made an effort to free himself from the morbid ideas which enveloped him like a web and controlled his natural faculties.

'Of course, there's my father, I know that; but he sent me here, and approves of the life I am leading.'

'Does he know and approve of your committing suicide; and if he behaves foolishly, does that justify your acting criminally? Are you compelled to do wrong because he is silly enough to say you may? Rather, does not your own knowledge of right tell you to do what is in your eyes likely to preserve his honour and secure him from remorse? Have you no better feeling of filial love and respect than to accelerate the punishment of your father's folly? Do you wish me to believe that when you drink a poison, that you know is to kill you in seven years, you excuse the act because your father approves of it?'

'Upon my soul, Vane, I have never thought of my father in the matter.'

'That is an admission. It is hard to wring the truth from such stubborn hearts as yours. You admit, then, that your father is concerned in the way you go to the devil, and that the way you have chosen for yourself is not to his advantage?'

Roland nodded, and hung his head sullenly. This old trick of flogging him with his own whip was to be played again, he thought.

'That is one person. Now, do you remember telling me last night that you loved Folly with all your heart and soul?'

'Yes; and I say so now, Dick.'

'And mean it?'

'Yes; and if I never was anything but a trifler in other matters, I am sincere in this.'

'I thought so last night. You seemed to me earnest then, and I think so now.'

'Thank you, Dick.'

'And so you see we have arrived at a total of two people who are concerned in your salvation—leaving out of the account such persons as Madge and me, and a Being not always to be forgotten.'

'If these thoughts would only occur to me as they do to you, I should never go wrong. I couldn't do wrong, if I had only some one near me to hint at my obligations and all that, and just remind me that I am going out of the rectilinear.'

'We shall speak of that presently.'

'You are a dear old fellow. I begin to breathe freer five minutes after you have been in the room. Just tell me what I am to do, Dick.'

'Well, to finish one subject before beginning another, what I want you to do is to promise me, upon your honour as a gentleman, never to touch vermouth or anything like it again.'

'But supposing a lot of fellows are drinking it, and they say, "Here, Aveling, old man, drink with us."'

'And supposing you are manly enough to reply, "Old man, I thank you all the same, but I prefer bitter beer," will you lose their esteem? If you would, their esteem is only worth losing.'

'Dick, as I'm a gentleman, I'll never touch the stuff again.'

'Jot it down in your betting-book, Roland; that seems to be the book in which gentlemen register their only inviolable pledges.'

'I will. And now let us talk of Folly.

Tell me all you think of her. Didn't you ask me for her address in the middle of the night, or did I dream that you did? Where have you been this morning?'

'To see Folly.'

'I hope she wasn't rude to you.'

'She was not very polite, I must confess.'

Vane's grave face lapsed into a smile as he remembered the message which Miss Clip did not deliver.

'One must make allowances for clever people, you know,' urged Roland. 'You consider her a great actress, don't you?'

'No. I don't know whether she can act at all. Acting, as I understand it, is the impersonation of a borrowed character. I imagine that Folly merely represents her own character and disposition.'

'Ah, I dare say you're right. But I'm sorry she was rude to you. Perhaps she didn't mean it?'

'It is more likely that she did. However, I did not go to examine her manners. I went to see if she was a good girl.'

'Well?' asked Roland, eagerly.

'I saw a proof of filial devotion in her which should be a lesson to you.'

'I have lots to learn, I know. What was it?'

'She did not wish it to be known.'

'Ah, she has some queer notions about her father, if that old lunatic is her father. I have asked her over and over again to let me place him in a proper asylum, you know, but she's deaf to reason.'

'She must love you deeply to forgive such a proposal. Nothing but death will separate her from him.'

'I suppose not; and, come to think of it, I ought not to have made the suggestion. What a thoughtless beggar I am!'

'You have taken the fact that they are inseparable thoroughly into consideration?'

'Oh yes. I made up my mind that she would not let the old man go away.'

'Before you told her you loved her?'

'Yes.'

Roland looked at Vane, wondering what he was driving at now.

'She has accepted your offer?'

'Yes, yes,' Roland replied, rather nervously, with a faint suspicion of what was to come. 'Yes, we were talking about taking a house and buying a pony-carriage last night.'

'I did not know matters had gone so far.

Well, Roland, I congratulate you, for I believe Folly to be as good a girl as ever lived. In her you will find one who will be the guide and counsellor you need; and, as for her love—Ah, a woman who can love a father as she loves hers must love her husband——'

'Husband, Dick?' Roland said, interrupting Vane.

'Yes. What mistake is there in that?'

'Only this—I have no intention of marrying Folly.'

'Then what do you intend doing?' Vane asked, sharply.

'Why, we—we intend going on just as we are.'

'I don't understand you. Speak plainly.'

'I have told Folly that the difference in our position prevented my making her my wife.'

'When did you tell her that?'

'Last night. She was very angry at first. I think she suspected me of dishonourable intentions, you know. She wouldn't come out between the acts—that is how it was you found me alone. But when I told her that I intended loving her in a platonic way, you know, she forgave me, and accepted my offer of the house and ponies.'

'That was after she had seen me?'

'Yes.'

Richard Vane reflected for some moments in silence. Certain features of this affair were inexplicable to him, but he attributed that fact to the mystification in which Roland had enveloped it, and not to those sinister motives of revenge which prompted Folly. He concluded that Folly had accepted a reconciliation with Roland, and agreed to the absurd scheme he suggested as a temporary means of securing him to herself.

'If we both agree to an innocent friendship, I cannot see who is to blame me,' said Roland.

'Of course you can't. You cannot see, also, that you are acting like a fool. Are you a Plato? You, who cannot see that it is wrong to commit suicide, are you to be trusted to keep within the cold, passionless circle of self-restraint. Tell me this, Plato—how did you part with your friend last night after offering house and ponies—did you offer to kiss?' Roland coloured to the temples. 'Had you ever done so before? Bah! your silence answers me. Roland, if I had not known you a year ago I should doubt if you ever had been manly; if I didn't know that you are besotted with vermouth and quack medicines I should think you out of your mind now; if I hadn't your promise to cease poisoning your body, I should despair of you having manly sentiments in the future.'

'What am I to do ? I feel I have been in error. Only tell me what I should do, and I will try and behave as a man should.'

'Do one of two things : take the next packet to America — Australia — anywhere away, and never see Folly again, or down upon your knees and ask her to be your wife.'

'Leave her—impossible !'

'Well !'

'Make her my wife—she is a burlesque actress !'

Vane jumped up, caught Roland by the arm, and, facing him round to the glass, asked :

'And what are you ?'

CHAPTER XVIII.

A POINT GAINED.

Y a vigorous effort, such as a sleeper makes to escape the clogging effects of nightmare, Roland aroused himself from the torpor into which he had sunk, and exulted once more in a sense of freedom and self-reliance and in the possession of active strength. Possibly he was weak and helpless as ever; but at least he was free from that debasing consciousness of weakness which precludes a man from attempting any healthy exertion.

He felt he might retrieve his lost ground by a step in the right direction, and that step he resolved to make. He would palter no more with the serious affairs of life; he would guide his actions solely by his own perception of right and wrong; he would do his utmost to deserve his own respect—setting up dear old Dick as his model, and doing as he believed Dick would do in parallel circumstances. He had given his word to drop vermouth, and small as that concession to the demands of virtue had been, it was still of appreciable worth as a beginning of better things.

To fly the country, with the determination of never again seeing Folly, was a course he could not bring himself to think of seriously. It would break his heart to leave her, and if he were ten thousand miles away he could think of her none the less. He doubted—and very justly—if his courage would sustain a long absence; in all probability his first act upon landing in America would be to take a berth in the next homeward-bound vessel. Besides these considerations, it seemed to him, in his present exaltation of courage, a sneaking and pusillanimous way of getting out of a difficulty. On the other hand, to marry Folly, in defiance of the conventional dictates of society, and simply because it was right to marry the woman he loved, was decidedly heroic. And so, before Vane had exhausted his arguments to show that a man must do not what is expedient but what is right, Roland had firmly determined to do his duty in the manner most agreeable to his inclinations.

Having come to this conclusion, he was anxious naturally to let Folly know as quickly as possible of the alteration in his character which gave him so much satisfaction. But great as this interest in his own affairs was he forgot them entirely, and was concerned only for Folly when he met her at night.

The girl was pale, and her manner grave and *distrait*—signs of distress which appealed directly to the generosity of Roland's disposition.

Vane had rightly doubted Folly's ability to represent any character but her own. It was with an effort she concealed her dislike to Roland; it would have required still greater exertion to simulate pleasure in his company, an exertion of which her mind was not at present capable.

'What is the matter, Folly dear?' Roland asked, with tender earnestness. 'You look pale and serious; and what has happened to your hand?'

'My hand—oh, that is nothing; and my

pale and serious face—that is nothing also. You have seen your friend since he called upon me?'

'Richard Vane? Yes, but——'

She interrupted him with a short laugh, and said, harshly:

'I suppose you think I have got no more than I might expect by taking care of my father against your reasonable advice, and so ought to take my punishment cheerfully as a thing of course?'

'I don't think anything so cruel, Folly. I have been heartless, and spoken unfeelingly of your father to you, I know, but I repent heartily; and now that my eyes are opened I see how beautiful your behaviour to him has been.'

Folly looked at him with curiosity.

'And as for what happened this morning,' he continued, 'I know nothing of it beyond the fact that something did occur which you wished should not be known.'

'Is that all he told you?'

'All. I don't want to know what happened. I only want you to tell me if I can do anything to lessen your distress, dear.'

'But you said your eyes had been opened,'

said Folly, disregarding all but her own thread of thought. 'Who opened them?'

'Vane. I—I—well, Folly, I told him that I had advised you to part with your father.'

'And what did he say?'

'He said you must love me very deeply to forgive me that.'

Folly took time to consider what she heard. Then she said:

'Did he tell you the message I sent him?'

'He said you were not very polite; but that makes no difference to Dick. He looks right under the surface before he judges; he wouldn't undervalue a diamond because its surface was unpolished. But your hand, Folly dear, is it much hurt?'

'No, no, no; a scratch; nothing at all,' Folly answered, waving her hand impatiently. 'I want to know more about this friend. What did he come to me for?'

'He wanted to find out if you were a good girl.'

'Well?' she asked, defiantly.

'He believes there is no better woman in the world than you. He showed me that you are ten thousand times better than I am. He made me see that you deserved the reverent love of an honest man, and not the childish mockery of love I had offered. He opened my eyes to my own faults by pointing to your virtues.'

Folly was perplexed. She had thought of Vane as a self-seeking man, and could not readily accept him in the truer character.

'I perceive now that to continue our intimacy on the footing I proposed is an impossibility, and that to attempt it is to jeopardise your happiness and honour.'

'I see. He wants you to leave me.'

'Yes; he insists upon my quitting England at once, or——' He stopped as Folly burst into a derisive laugh. She checked herself abruptly, to repeat his last word :

'Or what?' she asked.

'Or make you my wife?'

Folly was thrown into doubt again.

'And what answer have you given him?'

'None. It remains for you to decide. I have come here to ask you to be my wife. What answer shall I give him, Folly dear?'

'Supposing I decline?'

Roland's heart sank within him at this unanticipated suggestion. He looked at Folly's still imperturbable face with growing alarm.

'Supposing I decline to be your wife?' she repeated.

They were walking. He stopped suddenly, as if the idea of losing her had deprived him of power to move, and, speaking low in deep emotion, said, hurriedly:

'Oh, Folly, do not give me that answer. I cannot live without you—at least, I feel as if it were impossible that I should. You do not know how I love you; I myself never knew how deeply until now when I tried to realise what I should be without you. For Heaven's sake do not refuse me. Vane said I should go down on my knees to ask you, but I did not recognise the significance of his words. Believe me, I feel now my own unworthiness. I ask you to accept me for what I shall be rather than what I am. I have given my word of honour to live a conscientious and good life; will you help me to live wisely also, and trust to my love for your happiness?'

They walked on slowly. Folly remaining silent, Roland said, in a firmer voice than she had yet heard:

'Answer me, Folly, at once. I am no longer a contemptible trifler; I am a man, and I love you.'

'If I refuse you, what will happen?'
'I must leave you.'
'When?'
'This evening.'
'And when will you return?'
'Never, if Heaven grants me strength to remember your happiness and forget my own.'

'And supposing I accept to be your wife?' Folly said, in a tone as cold as that in which she had put the other contingency.

'I shall do all that I can to make you happy, and to——'

'I am not thinking of that. Your father —you told me last night that it would break his heart if you married me.'

'I couldn't tell him directly. I suppose it would not actually break his heart—that is only a *façon de parler;* but it would be a severe mortification to him. As you do not wish to relinquish the stage, we can easily conceal our marriage for the years the dear old gentleman has to live. By the time he is called away you will perhaps like to retire and take your place as my wife in Aveling Hall.'

Folly's eyes glistened—Roland thought with the prospect he suggested.

'Is that not also a *façon de parler* to say our marriage would mortify him?'

'No, indeed; it would be the severest blow that could be inflicted upon him. I believe he would sooner see me dead than married as he considers badly. That mortification can be easily spared him, and you know, Folly, that I do not share his opinion. I consider you honour me by being my wife.'

'But he would not. He would sooner see you dead, you say.'

'I believe he would. It has been the hope of his life that I should take his place in society. It gave him the greatest distress to think I should marry Vane's sister.'

They walked for some distance in silence, then Roland said:

'Your love for your own father will tell you how necessary it is for me to respect the feelings of mine. He has been most indulgent and kind to me. It does not matter to me what other people think or say—I can defend myself and you; but him I am bound to consider.'

'But are you certain it would grieve him so deeply?'

'If you knew him you would not have to ask that question. You will not wish to change your name while you remain on the stage, and it cannot be very many years that the dear old dad——'

Roland paused. He did not like to speculate upon his father's death.

'I would like the dear old gentleman's last days to be happy,' he said, with a sigh.

Folly thought of her father's last days.

'You see the expediency of a secret marriage?' Roland continued.

'Yes, yes.'

'And will you be my wife, Folly dear?'

She answered in a firm voice:

'Yes.'

CHAPTER XIX.

VANE'S PROJECT.

RICHARD VANE did not see Roland until the following morning at eleven o'clock. Then he found him buried in the 'Stones of Venice.' Roland was 'going in' for rectitude with impetuosity. He had abstained from liqueurs, and limited himself to a pint of Baum the night before; he had gone to bed at midnight or a little later, and risen at seven. Finding ice on the top of the water-ewer, he had considered it a good thing to have a cold bath, and he had taken it and shivered for it. He had resolutely eaten a good breakfast, and since then got through four-and-twenty pages of the work before mentioned.

Spasmodic virtue was more objectionable

to Vane's mind than spasmodic vice, since it too clearly indicated a normal condition of a less desirable kind. But he said nothing now to discourage Roland. He wished to restore to its usual vigour the vitality which was but just returning to his friend's conscience, and did all he could to encourage him.

He listened sedately to the sweeping strictures made upon the 'Stones of Venice,' merely remarking, when his opinion upon them was appealed to, that the argument might be just, but that he had never found himself capable of criticising twenty-four pages of Mr. Ruskin's works in so short a space of time.

'Ah, that's the way with you giants, you always are slow,' said Roland, with a wave of his hand; and so dismissing that subject, he went on to speak of his own personal affairs.

Vane heard that Folly had consented to marry Roland, and had agreed to a secret marriage in consideration of Sir Andrew's feelings. He hated the name of secrecy, especially when the concealment was between people so nearly allied as father and son; but he saw that in the present case he could not be exacting. He believed that the plant he had under cultivation would grow straight and strong in time, but he dared not train it too closely at first, for fear of checking its growth. He conjectured that Roland's impulsiveness would lead him to confess everything the first time he found his father in an amiable mood, and there the secrecy would end.

He gathered from what he heard that Roland had taken a manlier position in his intercourse with Folly, and that pleased him. He was willing now that the young fellow should go alone, and obtain strength by exercise. Avoiding the didactic style, he told him in a few words all that he thought and felt, and concluded by saying that probably they should not meet again for some days.

'You can't tell how delighted I am to hear you talk like this, Dick,' said Roland. 'It's just like the old times. You never did begrudge praise; that's what makes your severity so telling, I expect. I'm going quite straight now—you trust me. Yes, I was manlier last evening; I felt more like —like clearing the hedges and going home with a whole skin, you know. God bless you, old man! Heaven knows in what mud I should not now be sticking but for your counsel. But what do you mean by running away so soon? You're not obliged to go back to Tangley before Sunday, are you?'

'No.' Vane smiled.

'Well, then, stop with me. I'll start you off in time for the morning show—I beg your pardon, I mean the first service.'

'I shall not return to Tangley—except possibly for a few hours to finish up affairs there.'

'Not return to Tangley! Where on earth are you going, then? Roland asked, in astonishment.

'I have been looking at a house in Spitalfields, and if I can come to terms with the landlord I shall probably go there.'

Richard Vane filled his pipe as he spoke; Roland looked at him in astonishment for a moment, and then asked for an explanation.

Having scratched a match and lit his tobacco, Vane recounted his reasons for resignation. Then he said:

'What I shall do in London is not definite yet awhile. I have just enough money to support Madge and myself with economy.'

'Poor Madge!' thought Roland, heartstricken. 'How different from the life we planned together! 'Poor dear Madge!' He kept his eyes on the ground as he said: 'What do you think of working at, Dick?'

'Anthing that comes to hand, Roley. If I can show people where their shoes pinch, and how they may contrive to walk in comfort, it will be worth something. There are plenty of men and women in London, and among them I shall find my work. Madge is lovely with children.'

A tear sprang into Roland's eye as he leaned with his elbows on his knees looking down at the carpet. 'Madge is lovely with children,' he repeated to himself. It was with the children of other women she was to be gentle and sweet—she must be a mother to them, with Rachel's unsatisfied yearnings at her heart.

'Do you know Spitalfields?' Vane asked, looking at a little chart drawn on the back of an envelope—his *agenda* for all sorts of facts and fancies. Roland shook his head. He couldn't speak; his heart, which had been frozen by selfishness, melted and bled now. 'Poor Madge!' were the only words his thoughts could form.

'It is a queer old place,' continued Vane, intent upon his chart, 'still bearing traces of the Huguenot refugees who settled there; weavers, with old French names, make silk in the garrets and keep pigeons in the cock-lofts. There's quite a large garden, with high walls, behind the house I want, and in the middle of it a mulberry tree stands and defies the soot of centuries—the landlord assures me it bears excellent fruit. One might dispute the miracle of Pyramus and Thisbe in accounting for the berries of that tree losing their original colour.'

Roland pictured Madge trying to grow in the grimy garden the pet annuals she cherished in Tangley, trying to keep her morning dresses white and pure—trying to forget what was lost to her.

'Sunday must be a busy day there. Petticoat Lane runs along here to the west; Club Row lies to the north; Brick Lane and Whitechapel border our eastern frontier; and Shoreditch with Bethnal Green complete our environment.'

'Great heavens, Dick! think what you are doing,' cried Roland looking up. 'All the thieves in London live there.'

'I am afraid not,' Vane replied, shaking his head. 'London is a large city. You know Shelley's comparison. I fear there are as few virtuous corners here, as in the city he compares it with.'

'It's all well enough for you—you always did go in for disagreeable jobs that no one else would touch. You're a man; but, but——'

'Madge!' said Vane, supplying the name which Roland scarcely dared to speak. 'Well, she's a woman, and a good woman.'

*   *   *   *   *

Roland told Folly at night of his conversation with Vane, explaining the sacrifice the vicar was making.

'If you could see him among the flowers in his garden, and knew what delight he takes in the pleasures of retirement, you would understand what it is he relinquishes. He finds a charm there even in wet weather. I have seen him walking round the garden in a rainy evening, with his shoulders a little bent and his hands behind him—so—noticing the freshened leaves of the little plants, and listening to the chattering of the sparrows in the ivy. And then to think of his giving up all that he likes to live in the worst part of London, among Jews and thieves, with nothing but smoke in the fine weather, and nothing but filthy mud in the wet time.

And then the work he has undertaken. At Tangley there were only clean, respectable poor people, and the church he preached in was like a pretty toy. All that he had to do was to preach a sermon there on Sundays. He will find it hard to get people to listen to him here—and will be laughed at. Ah, he is a dear, good old fellow!'

Folly nodded her head. She doubted Vane's honesty no longer.

'Do you think he likes the country as we like London?' she asked.

'He likes it as you like London.'

'I never saw anything in the country so pretty as the scenery on the stage. The people are untidy and stupid, and there are workhouses and prisons, and—oh, I hate the country!'

'And he hates London. But he loves the people—all people, Folly, and it gives him the greatest happiness to make their troubles less. He would sooner carry a burden than see another weighed down under it.'

'That don't seem real—for a man. Are all parsons like that?'

'No. I suppose there would not be any toy churches if they were.'

'What are parsons for?'

'To help people to be good, to teach them to do right.'

'Then why has he given up being a parson?'

'Because the people that most need teaching and helping don't go to church, I expect; and because he couldn't believe all the things a parson has to teach.'

'Can't a parson teach just what he thinks is right?'

'No; he must teach certain things that are set down by law.'

'What, the law that is made by members of Parliament—your father, and men like him, that you told me about the other day?'

'Yes.'

'Then he doesn't believe in members of Parliament?'

'I can't say that. He certainly does not think that everything they have done is right.'

'So he is a Republican like me, eh?'

Roland laughed at the girl's earnest manner. It was so odd to think of an uneducated and beautiful young girl taking interest in politics. She repeated her question, impatiently.

'Well, he has Republican ideas, certainly,' he admitted.

'What ideas?'

'He thinks that all good men are equal—which is sheer absurdity, you know.'

'That is what you think. I want to know what he thinks. Go on.'

'Then he thinks it is wrong for any man to live idly upon the wealth produced by those who work.'

'What men are they?'

'Well, I dare say my father may be classed among them; so may I; so may nearly all the fellows you see in the stalls. Now, my father, for example, owns his wealth because he is fortunate enough to be the descendant of a man who had all Tangley and Mayford——'

'Mayford?'

'Yes, Mayford, and Crewe given him by the king a long, long while ago. This land my father lets in farms to men who cultivate it and pay him rent with the money they get for their crops. If the crops are good the farmer lives comfortably and gives his servants good wages, so it's good for everybody after all, and I don't see who can find fault with the arrangements.'

'But if the crops are bad?' suggested Folly.

'Why then the farmer has to pinch a bit, and his servants can't get so much work, you see.'

'Yes, I see; it is good for your father always, it is good for the farmer sometimes, and now and then it is very bad for the labourers.'

'Oh, in bad times there is always a good deal of charity about—blankets and soup——'

'For some, and workhouses and prisons for others,' said Folly, fiercely, with the evil look in her eyes.

Roland was frightened by her expression.

'Let us talk of something else,' he said. 'People always feel uncomfortable when they begin to talk about politics. Even you, Folly, look angry.'

'Never mind my looks,' said Folly, trying to soften her tone as she recollected the necessity to conceal her feelings. 'It is better to talk of these things than rubbish. Mr. Vane thinks it is unjust to have idle masters and suffering slaves.'

'He does not go so far as to class all gentlemen as tyrants and all working men as slaves, but I believe he thinks that the present arrangement is wrong and unjust.

But he himself is not right in all things, Folly dear; there must always be two classes, the rich and the poor. Now, I am not a Republican.'

'Of course not. You do not want to work.'

Roland laughed at the *coup*. Folly laughed also, but her pleasure was of a malicious kind.

' I dare say Vane thinks that parsons who are paid to do good and don't do it, who only amuse or befool a parcel of silly people, are also to be classed with those who live idly by the work of others, and adds that to his reason for resigning his vicarship.'

Folly was silent for a few minutes; she was thinking about Vane.

'That good man—your friend—Mr. Vane,' she said presently, 'he believes in the Bible?'

'Well, he has scruples about that. There never was such a fellow for finding fault with things which everyone else believes perfect.'

'What scruples?'

'I can't explain quite. He does not think that all in it is to be taken as our guide; but that again is wrong, for everyone admits it is the best work that was ever written.'

'Oh yes, I know that, and I believe it,' Folly replied, with emphasis. Then, after a moment's pause, she said: 'He does not disbelieve, "And thine eye shall not pity; but life shall go for life, eye for eye, tooth for tooth, hand for hand, foot for foot," does he?'

'Why, that's the very thing he would not agree with,' answered Roland, not a little astonished at the girl's Biblical knowledge.

'Why?'

'Because he believes it our duty to forgive, to be merciful to those who have been unmerciful to us. That is a doctrine of revenge which he is perpetually striving to undo. Vengeance he regards as wicked, cruel, and unjust.'

'I don't!' Folly said, with energetic force. 'No one could make me believe the Bible wrong.'

'It is the same with other institutions, Folly; we agree with them when their principles don't oppose our feelings. Revenge is sweet, I say, although I certainly agree with Vane in the abstract, that it is inconsistent with Christianity. But I wish you would talk to him as you have talked to me. He would think better of you than ever. Shall I ask him to dine with us one evening?'

'Oh no—no, no, no!' Folly answered, sharply. She wanted a cruel man for a friend now, not a merciful one. 'No, no—I hate him. I won't see him. I'll be rude to him.'

'All right, darling; I won't ask him if you do not wish it,' Roland replied, attributing her repugnance to caprice.

Later in the evening she said to Roland:

'How soon can we be married?'

'I don't exactly know. A few days, I think.'

'Then we will be married in a few days,' she answered.

CHAPTER XX.

PREPARING FOR HAPPINESS.

ROLAND applied for a licence the following day.

He had no objection to hurrying the ceremony to a conclusion; haste suited his impulsive disposition. Having set his foot on the path of virtue, he wished to rush along over the ground headlong, lest he might, by delay, be tempted to stray from it again. A comfortable home to live in after his marriage was a necesssity, however, which could not be overlooked even in this impetuous advance.

'And now,' he said, after his return from Doctors' Commons, 'the next thing is to look for a house.'

'A house?' Folly repeated, looking up in surprise.

It seemed that she had even less prudential forethought than he.

'Why, yes, Folly; we can't live in hotels; and you know that circumstances prevent my living with you in Lambeth Road.'

He had not for a moment anticipated living in the same house with her father; but he made this reference to Lambeth Road as a suggestion to Folly that she also would be unable to live there after their marriage—a fact which he thought she might have lost sight of in her careless consideration of the future. Despite his strong desire to regard Folly's feeling, and to like her father—as much as he could—he was heartily grateful that the old man's repugnance offered a bar to their closer connection. It pleased him to think that Folly would be happier when she saw less of her father. Certainly they could not live all together in the same house.

It seemed as if this consequence had, in reality, escaped Folly. She pushed her glass aside—they were dining together—rested her elbow on the table and her chin in her hand, and looked absently before her.

'Has it not occurred to you that we shall have to take a house?' Roland asked.

She shook her head in silence, still occupied with her meditation.

'You see the necessity, I hope?'

She nodded her head, and then looked at Roland with a strange expression in her face, which he could not understand. There was quick excitement in her eyes as she said:

'Yes, yes; we must have a house to go to after the wedding. Where shall it be?'

'I have been to a house agent, and got a list of houses,' answered Roland, flattering himself on his superior prevision. 'Of course a man thinks of these things. We can go and see some of them to-morrow.'

Folly acceded to the suggestion readily, and the next morning and afternoon they devoted to looking at the houses on Roland's list. A pleasant little detached villa in the Clapham Road was the most suitable they could find. In this selection Folly was less difficult to please than Roland. The first they saw 'would do,' she thought, until he pointed out the objections to it. Eager and excited as she was at times in speaking of the forthcoming ceremony, she seemed entirely careless as to what followed. This apathy chilled Roland, and was the more surprising to him as he remembered the pleasure she had taken on a previous evening in talking of her pony-carriage and future *ménage*.

The Clapham villa had a coach-house and stable, and these advantages Roland pointed out, without, however, exciting Folly's interest to the degree he expected. Behind the house was a tolerably large flower-garden, with a lawn, protected from the observation of neighbours by high fruit-tree-covered walls.

'It will be very pretty in the summer time, and we can have jolly garden-parties on a small scale, you know. We can have our little receptions on Sunday; and, oh, how lovely you will look, floating about on the green turf with lots of geraniums and bright flowers around you!'

'When the summer comes,' Folly answered, coldly.

She seemed more pleased with the arrangement of the rooms than with anything else.

There were two large rooms on the first floor, communicating with each other.

'This front room shall be ours, Folly. It is spacious and convenient; and this other,' he said, taking her into the adjoining apartment, 'this shall be your own private room, where you can retire to study or do what you will.'

'I can have this all to myself?'

'Yes; no one shall go into it but you and your maid—unless you choose to invite your husband to see you there sometimes.'

'I shall invite you,' she said, quietly.

'You darling!' he said, stepping towards her. He would have taken her in his arms and kissed her; but, as if by accident, she turned her back on him and walked to the window.

Had he seen the look of sickening repugnance on her face he would have known it was not by accident she escaped him.

'You like the house, Folly, and think it will do?' Roland asked, when they left the first floor and descended.

'Yes, it will do capitally. When can we come into it?'

'I will see the proprietor. It is in good order, and I dare say there will be no obstacle to prevent us taking immediate possession. Then, as soon as the furniture is in, we can occupy our home. But it will be difficult to find servants at such short notice.'

'There need be no delay on that account. Clip will settle all that.'

'But she will be doubly occupied when you leave Lambeth Road. Of course, you will keep on your apartments there. That arrangement will not be altered.'

'Oh, that will be all right. I will see to that. You look after the house and the furniture.'

'You should have a maid besides those necessary for the general domestic work.'

'Yes, yes, yes! And now, when do you think we can be married?'

'Within the week. But we need not wait. We could be married before, and live in an hotel until the house is ready.'

Against this proposal Folly set her face emphatically. She would on no account be married until the house was ready for their reception.

Few difficulties are not to be overcome by ready money. The personal investigations which a prudent landlord makes before accepting a tenant are not found necessary in the case of one who proves his respectability by paying in advance; and the press of business which prevents a furniture dealer from executing orders without delay does not preclude him from accepting a contract to furnish a house from garret to basement in three days when his payment is dependent on such despatch; and so Roland received the key of the villa, and saw the bare house transformed to a well-appointed home all within the space of five days.

He took an apartment in the neighbourhood that he might superintend the arrangement of the rooms, and went into the details of the affair with an energetic spirit which not even Folly's indifference could damp. Every evening he told her of the progress made during the day, but she gave no more than a forced expression of pleasure. She admitted that her father's health occupied her thoughts; he had not been so well; and to this fact Roland attributed her coldness to himself. She was extremely reticent about John Morrison; her silence was a tacit impeachment of Roland's sympathy, which he knew too well deserved suspicion. He tried his utmost to assure her of his kindlier feelings towards the old man, but she did not want his sympathy, and encouraged her own harshest thoughts of his motives and disposition. That she had been compelled to call in a physician and engage a professional attendant for her father was all he learnt.

'I hope, Folly dear, that you will accept my help soon, and that I may be of service to you in lessening your father's sufferings,' he said kindly. 'I wish I could do something now.'

'You can do nothing yet,' she replied.

'Perhaps you would like to postpone the marriage until this attack passes over!'

'No. I want the marriage to take place quickly,' she said; and then, with impatience, she added, 'How much longer do those furnishing people intend to keep us waiting?'

'They will leave to-night. The little house looks beautiful. Would you like to see it to-morrow?'

'Yes. There may be something I wish to add. We will go to-morrow morning. You can call for me. My father is obliged to keep his room, and will not see you.'

Early the next day Roland called for Folly, and took her to the villa. She was pale and silent. In reply to his questions respecting her father's health, she said:

'He is still very ill, but no worse.'

The gates and railings before the house were still wet with paint; the semicircular turf was newly mown, and the fresh gravel on the carriage drive well rolled; the house itself was bright and cheerful to the eye.

Roland took the key from his pocket and opened the door; then he conducted Folly over the house, showing her the well-filled cellars, the kitchens, glittering with a long array of bright copper pots and pans; the drawing-room, with its light, elegant furniture and water-colours; the dining-room, with its darker and warmer decorations; the little conservatory, fragrant and bright with spring flowers from Covent Garden.

Folly looked at these things as she might at a book of poems which she could not hope to read; she looked at them, and listened to Roland's lively chat, as, with hopeful enthusiasm, he suggested the many happy events that might take place in their house, with unconcealed melancholy. She spoke scarcely a single word. Despite the absorbing pleasure of showing all he had done for her happiness, Roland remarked her dejection.

'Poor girl!' said he to himself; 'she cannot forget her father. Well, well; she will enjoy this home when the poor old man is gone.'

They went upstairs. Folly passed hastily through the first room into that which was to be her own private room, and found herself in a boudoir which exceeded all she had ever seen on the stage or elsewhere in beauty, and drew from her an involuntary exclamation of delight. All that could be done by the upholsterer to make the room perfect had been done.

The centre of the room was unencumbered with furniture, that Folly might rehearse there if she would, and see the effects she made in the long mirrors placed between the windows. A beautiful Persian carpet was spread over the pale blue carpet, and from above there hung a candelabra of Venetian glass. The hangings of the windows, corresponding with the coverings of the chairs, were of blue satin, covered with white lace. Half-a-dozen differently shaped fauteuils stood near the tables by the walls. A pair of charming French cabinets filled two corners; the other two contained brackets, on which stood spring lilies in blue Wedgwood pots. The surface of the walls was broken up with a few pictures and two or three mirrors and candelabra brackets.

'Do you like your room, Folly?' asked Roland, catching her expression of pleasure.

'It is very beautiful,' she answered.

'It is not half so lovely as I would make it if I could. Nothing in the world seems to me good enough for your use.'

Folly made a step forward towards the cabinets, and then, checking herself, as if suddenly recalling her previous feelings, she turned round abruptly.

'Let us leave this room. Let us go away,' she said quickly.

Roland opened the door, and she passed out rapidly.

'There is nothing now to prevent our being married, is there?' she asked, soon after.

'Nothing. Every arrangement is complete, except—well, I shall have one little surprise for your wedding morning.'

'What kind of a surprise?'

'One that will give you pleasure, I hope.'

When they reached the street-door, and were about to leave the house, Folly said, with less firmness in her voice than was usual with her:

'Everything is finished here, you tell me— nothing more has to be brought in?'

'No. You have arranged with the servants?'

'Yes,' she replied, avoiding Roland's eyes. 'Yes; that reminds me. I want you to give me the key—that key you have in your hand.'

'I see; you will have to admit the servants and give them instructions. Is that it?'

'Yes, yes.'

'But cannot I relieve you of that trouble?'

'No; I would rather do it myself. Give me the key, if you please.'

'Certainly,' he replied. It seemed to him that her hand trembled as she took the key from his hand.

'Poor girl! her father's illness has quite unnerved her,' he said to himself.

CHAPTER XXI.

CORRESPONDENCE.

FOLLY was anxious to return to her father, and declined to take lunch with Roland; so he, having taken her to Lambeth Road, went on to the Corinthus to lunch, and answer what correspondence might be there awaiting him.

He found a letter from his father, forwarded from Grandison Chambers, and another from Vane, written in the club.

He opened his father's letter first, not without compunctious fear, and read it, commenting on it as he went:

'MY DEAR BOY,
    'I conclude by your neglect of me that you are enjoying yourself greatly.

['Hang it! I ought to have answered that last letter.'] Well, well, old men must not be exacting; they must content themselves with keeping their boys out of harm's way, and making them happy, without expecting any return of their affection. ['Now, that's the old dad all over. If one doesn't answer his letter the very moment it is received, he concludes that he is forgotten and neglected because of his old age. Why, he ought to know that I love him more every year of his life—and so he does, too.'] At present I console myself with the reflection that you are young, and the hope that I may be spared to see you outlive your thoughtlessness, but not your happiness. You will find that happiness is not inseparable from frivolity, and that you may derive equal pleasure and greater satisfaction from the higher occupations which come with maturity. ['The governor read the *Spectator* or *Tatler* before he wrote this, I know.'] I have especial reasons, just now, for wishing that the time when you will realise this fact is not far distant. At luncheon after the last bench meeting, Dr. Sturge gave us his confidential opinion that Mr. Falkland cannot outlive the autumn, and the question then arose as to who should represent the borough in Parliament. You may naturally conclude that I did not forget you. I said, what I felt to be true, that a better, a wiser, a more dashing, eloquent young fellow than you does not exist; and that if you were returned your voice in the House of Commons would make itself heard all over the country, and do more to revive the flagging spirit of Conservatism than all the bribery in the world. ['By George, I'd do my best! What an old trump the dad is! Yes, if I were in the House, I'd speak up and support all he has said of me.'] Our old friend the mayor supported me warmly, and assured me that if you would only go about among the county families you would undoubtedly win over all those who might be reluctant to give their voices for one of whom they knew so little. My dear boy, you know what my feelings towards you are; you know how proud I am of you; and so you will readily understand how I hope for a consummation which would make me the happiest and proudest old man in England.'

Roland laid the letter down. 'Poor old dad!—when he knows all!' he said.

The waiter announced that luncheon was ready. Roland nodded absently, and took up the letter again and read:

'With this brilliant prospect before you, you will see how providential was your escape from a *mésalliance*. Had you married Miss Vane it would have been impossible for you to expect recognition from influential friends—an impossibility rendered certain by the late behaviour of your old friend, Richard Vane, who, as you are perhaps aware, has thrown up his living, and openly professed opinions of a conscientious and anarchical character which——'

Roland wished to read no more. He closed the letter with a sigh, and drew up to the table. There he ate and thought, and found no pleasant savour.

'Happily he knows nothing of what is about to happen, and I pray to Heaven he never may.'

With this prayer Roland finished his reflections and his luncheon, and then opened Vane's letter. It contrasted oddly with the verbosity of Sir Andrew's:

'DEAR ROLAND,

'Where shall I find you? We are now settled in our new house, 53, Church Street, Spitalfields.

'Yours,

'DICK.'

Roland sat down at a table to answer these letters, undertaking first the more difficult one to his father. It was an unpleasant task to try and deceive one who was so good and generous to him, but it was necessary. Every word he wrote looked to him like a lie against which his heart revolted. Page after page of the club paper he wrote upon, crumpled up, and threw into the waste-paper basket. At length he gave up the task in disgust, determining to do to-morrow what he could nohow do to-day.

He wished to have Vane's advice on the subject, and for a moment meditated 'looking him up' in Spitalfields. But the letter indicated that Margaret was with him, and so he abandoned that idea. A meeting with her must be attended with mutual embarrassment and discomfort. Then, again, he knew exactly what advice he should get from Vane —advice to be true to his truthful instincts, and boldly tell his father all. That was what Vane himself would have done in his position; but his example could not in the present case be followed. Roland's soft, weak nature recoiled from the pain of giving pain.

He wrote a few lines to Vane, explaining why he had removed from his old chambers, and telling him of his approaching marriage.

In the evening he told Folly of Vane's letter, and his answer.

'Is it too late to ask him to the wedding?' she asked.

'No. A telegram to-morrow morning would probably find him. I thought you did not wish to see him.'

'I should like him to be at the wedding all the same.'

'I will send a message the first thing to-morrow morning. Nothing will please me better. It would seem incomplete if he were absent. I owe my happiness to him. And you must like him when you know him.'

So the next morning Richard Vane received a telegram from Roland. It ran thus:

'Folly wishes you to be present to-day. St. Olaph's, Brompton, twelve o'clock.

About the same time that this message

was handed to Vane, Banks presented Sir Andrew Aveling with the letters brought in by the first post. One endorsed 'Sir Aveling, Esq.,' he left to read last. The crabbed feminine hand in which the address was written and thin envelope suggested an appeal such as the baronet frequently received from needy women. He looked for his cheque-book before opening it; then he broke the cover and read:

'27, Lambeth Rd., S.E., Jenuary 27, 180070.

'MY DERE SIR,

'My Mistriss, Miss Folly, presents her complimens to you, and as she is going to be marryed to your son, Mr. Roland Aveling, Esq., to-morrow morning, the 28th, should be glad of your cumpany at their House, Thorn Villar, Clapham Rode, soon as convenyant, and begs me to say a train lieves Woking Station at 10.45 as will sute you.

'Hopein no offence, am yours respecfully,

'E. CLIP.

'Plese ekscuse mistakes.'

Under this composition Folly had written her name in large letters, with the customary flourish at the end.

CHAPTER XXII.

THE WEDDING OF ROLAND AVELING AND FOLLY MORRISON.

THE horizon was clear to Roland's perception on his wedding morning. That a storm might rise he was conscious; he feared that it must break upon him at no far distant date, but he felt sure of one day's unclouded happiness, and wantonly threw aside all considerations beyond the enjoyment of the hour.

At eleven o'clock Miss Clip opened the door of the house in Lambeth to Roland. She was greatly confused, and strove in vain to conceal her agitation. Poor woman! she found it impossible to serve her two friends faithfully. It was natural she should feel kindly towards the good-looking young gentleman who had given her so many tangible proofs of his generous disposition, and, knowing what trouble was in store for him, she wished, with all her heart, to warn him of his danger. But how could she do that and reconcile it with her allegiance to Folly, whose friendship was yet more valuable to her? She had, indeed, remonstrated with the girl in his behalf, and only desisted on being told, in sharp and unmistakable terms, to mind her own business. The business of Miss Clip's life was to accumulate money, and all her actions were governed by prudential considerations; nevertheless, as she looked into Roland's cheerful face, she felt she must save him at any sacrifice.

'I have come to take Folly away from you,' said he, gaily.

Miss Clip stammered a few incoherent syllables, and, her heart beating quickly, she was about to abandon reserve and give that simple advice to Roland which Mr. Punch offered 'to persons about to marry,' when she caught the sound of rustling silk behind her, and so stepped back silenced, to make way for Folly.

Folly was pale and grave; there was something deathly in the cold, impassive whiteness of her face. She was dressed entirely in black, which, by contrast, heightened the effect of her pallor. Roland stepped forward to meet her.

'You are not well, Folly dearest,' he said tenderly, as he pressed the gloved hand she allowed him to take.

She shrugged her shoulders, as if her health were a matter of indifference, and so dismissing the subject, said :

' Is the hansom waiting ?'

'No. I have brought a carriage, which I hope you will like better. A wedding present for my darling.'

He led the way to the door. In the road there stood a beautiful *bijou* phaeton, bright and shining as it had come from the coachbuilder's, with a rich fur rug upon the seat. A pair of bay ponies, with black and silver harness, were shaking their pretty heads and pawing the ground impatiently, restrained by a very small boy in a smart livery, who stood before them in a commanding pose with his arms crossed. A pair of snowy reins and a whip were ready for the driver's hand.

Here was the realisation of Folly's dream ; yet from her expression it seemed as if she were awaking from a dream to a barren and disappointing reality. It was, indeed, a mournful mockery of happiness to show her pleasures which she could not enjoy—it was as if a fine instrument were placed in the hands of an artist who had lost the sense of hearing. She stopped by the ponies to stroke their sleek sides; she noticed her initials upon the silver mountings of the harness; she looked at the diminutive servant in livery, who touched his hat to her respectfully; she saw all that might have filled her young soul with wild excitement, and she wished to weep away the load from her heart.

She stepped into the carriage and took the lower seat.

'You will drive, won't you?' Roland asked.

She shook her head, without speaking.

Roland put the rug over her, and, going round the carriage, took his place beside her. *Le géant*, as Roland had christened the mite in livery, left the ponies' heads and scrambled into his place as the vehicle dashed off.

'I am afraid your father is ill this morning, Folly,' said Roland, looking at Folly's pained face.

'Yes, he is ill. Do not speak to me,' she replied.

Roland did not interrupt her reflections, unable alike to fathom the secret of her distress or to offer consolation.

Folly sat back in her seat, her chin upon her breast, and her eyes oblivious of the things they saw.

Gradually a faint trace of colour came to her cheek, as they passed rapidly through the keen air, and her spirits revived.

'It is stupid to cry for what is not, and what cannot be,' she said to herself. 'Ponies and pretty houses are but playthings for fortunate children; only the silliest weep because they are not fortunate. And a friend all good and true, and unblemished and pure, does not live. Heaven would be jealous of him. Come, let me think of God, and the punishment He has put in my hands, and my father and Roland's father.'

Following this new train of thought, she presently said:

'When did you hear from your father last?'

'I had a letter from him yesterday, dear.'

'You didn't tell me. What did he say?'

'Nothing that would be pleasant to tell you, or you would have known it last night.'

'Anything to do with your father interests me. Tell me what he said.'

'Oh, the old story, you know—congratulated me on not marrying Miss Vane. And then the dear old gentleman is in a high state of delight with the prospect of getting me a seat in Parliament.'

'Could the husband of an actress get a seat in Parliament?'

'It would go against him at the election, I expect. But what does that matter to me? If I have you, dearest, I want nothing.'

'But your father——'

'He must never know. He may be wrong and prejudiced, but we must respect his feelings. I cannot forget that he is my father.'

'Nor I.'

They were silent after that, until, turning out of the Brompton Road, Roland said:

'That is the church, Folly, and there is old Dick waiting. See!'

'I am glad he has come; I want him to see it all.'

Richard Vane was standing before the church, his hands behind him. He came forward and offered his hand to Folly as the carriage drew up.

'We begin a long friendship to-day, I hope,' he said.

'I hope so,' she said, with much earnestness.

'I say, Dick,' said Roland, bustling round. 'A happy thought has just struck me. Instead of a snuffy old sexton doing the business, why shouldn't you give away the bride?'

'Because he does not believe as I believe,' said Folly, sharply.

'It is only a form, Folly dear. I thought —but, however——' Roland stammered.

'It is something more than a form to me,' she answered.

Roland, abashed by the rebuke, and unable to understand the exceptional severity of Folly's manner, did not reply; as they moved towards the church-door he offered his arm. Folly seemed not to notice the action; she kept her hands folded before her and her eyes in solemn awe upon the building she was about to enter. On the threshold she suddenly stopped, turning her eyes first to Richard Vane, and from him to Roland. Trembling violently, she caught their arms as if to restrain them from going farther.

With a reverence for the unknown God, such as only the greatest or the simplest minds can feel, she dared not enter His presence with the feeling which then agitated her heart—a feeling of remorseful pity for the man she was sacrificing to her purpose.

She did not know the cause from which her present hesitation sprang; she could not understand why her heart fainted at the prospect of taking this long-premeditated step.

'I have never been in a church. Give me time to compose myself,' she said, still trembling.

The womanly impulse passed away as if it had been the effect of physical weakness, rather than the cause of it; and centring her mind upon the religious duty before her, she regained strength, and her thoughts were exalted above mere personal considerations. The idea that in avenging her father's wrongs she was justified by Heaven, lifted her feelings to a level with those of the enthusiasts who have slaughtered their children from no higher motive.

It was not the savage instinct of retaliation—it was not even the animosity excited by the contemplation of her father's degradation—it was the feeling that she had to execute a divinely entrusted mission which restored her courage—the same feeling which had sustained her resolution in carrying out a vengeful purpose through all the opposing influences of a gentle and sweet nature—against all the naturally good and forgiving instincts of her heart.

She was, in short, as clearly a victim to ignorance as any Christian who ever tortured a heretic in the name of Heaven.

'I am ready now,' she said.

Roland stepped forward, and as he opened the door removed his hat.

Folly untied the strings of her bonnet.

'It is not necessary for you to do that,' he said, smiling at her simplicity.

'Why not?' she asked. 'If you uncover before God, should not I?'

Richard Vane took her bonnet. With her hands before her she walked up the aisle and stood before the altar, where the radiant light fell from the stained windows.

Beautiful she looked as a young saint standing there, with her pale creamy face, her rippling chestnut hair drawn off from her open brow, her lips a little parted, and her steadfast eyes wide open in reverential awe.

The ceremony was performed without interruption. There were no spectators. Folly did what she was told to do, and was married to Roland Aveling irrevocably.

CHAPTER XXIII.

AFTER THE WEDDING.

"YOU will return with us, Dick, and see our home. There is a front seat for you in the trap,' Roland said, when they left the church.

'I want you to come with us,' Folly added earnestly.

Richard Vane bowed, and presently took his seat in the phaeton. Folly declined to take the reins, and was scarcely less silent as they drove homewards than she had been in coming. Roland did his utmost to enliven her, but his efforts were futile, and met with no response. He became certain that 'something must be the matter,' and, wondering what it might be, grew silent also.

Richard Vane could understand that a girl

of deep feeling should regard the ceremony which had taken place with gravity, but her coldness towards Roland—the evident repugnance, indeed, with which she met his more tender overtures—astonished and alarmed him. Her expressed anxiety that he should accompany them to their home led him to anticipate that she intended to make a revelation of that which made her present behaviour mysterious. He waited anxiously.

A wedding is usually made to appear as much like a farce as possible; but anything more like the opening of a tragedy than the acting of the principal performer in this marriage would be difficult to conceive.

At Thorn Lodge *le géant* sprang down from his seat and opened the gate.

The ponies objected to the fresh paint, and refused to set their feet upon the new gravel, until Roland applied the whip smartly; then they made a dash that made Vane solicitous for Folly's safety, and called for a steady handling of the reins. Vane's back was to the house, and Roland's eyes were upon the ponies; so it happened that only Folly, sitting unmoved and collected in the seat beside her husband, caught sight of the pale, fair-faced, white-haired, portly old gentleman, who stood with his hat on watching their approach from the drawing-room window.

The door was opened by Miss Clip, who, quaking with fear, drew back and screened herself behind the door to the best of her ability as the party passed into the hall.

With a firm step Folly crossed straight to the drawing-room, opened the door, and walked in.

Resting one hand upon his stick and the other upon a table, stood the same portly old gentleman Folly had seen looking from the window. He looked straight at Folly, without moving a muscle of his face, and without attempting to remove his hat. She looked with equal fixity at him, and found in his face, now harsh with suppressed anger, a duplicate of the picture her imagination had presented of Sir Andrew Aveling.

For a dozen seconds they stood face to face thus.

Meanwhile in the hall Roland, speaking to Vane, said :

'I don't know what on earth is the matter with the poor girl to-day—I expect her father's very ill. Hang your hat on there, old man. She puzzles me fairly. Take off your coat.'

At this moment Folly came to the drawing-room door.

'A visitor is in this room—one that you know, I dare say. Come and introduce us to each other, Roland,' she said.

'A visitor!' Roland exclaimed, in suppressed astonishment.

The visitor announced himself in a hard, loud voice.

'My name is Andrew Aveling,' he said.

'Great Heavens — my father!' Roland murmured, and then looked in his old school-boy way to Vane for counsel.

Vane pointed to the door, and followed Roland into the drawing-room.

Folly stood six yards from Sir Andrew, facing him as he stood with his back to the window, in an erect easy position, nursing one hand within the other; pale still, but with no sign of emotion upon her face. Vane approached her, and took a position a little behind. Roland crossed the room towards his father.

'Sir, your hat is on. May I remind you that there is a lady in the room?' he said.

'Come no nearer,' said Sir Andrew, raising

his hand from the table. 'Before I acknowledge anyone in this room—before I acknowledge even my own son—I must learn who deserves my respect. In the first place, what is that woman?'

He glanced at Folly.

Roland hesitated, thinking how he might modify or tone down the facts which he feared must be revealed unless Folly or Dick came to his assistance. Folly responded to the quick inquiring glance he shot towards her, at once making the position less complicated.

'I can answer that question best,' she said 'My name is Folly; I was born in a workhouse. I was fostered by a harlequin, I was a scullery drab for seven years, and since then I've got my living by dancing in theatres and music-halls.'

Roland listened in silent amazement. This brief summary of her life's experiences was less astonishing to Sir Andrew, as he expected nothing but bravado and bold insolence from her.

The facts were none the less displeasing, however. Rapping his knuckles on the table beside him, he said, still frowning on his son:

'I ask you, sir, who is this woman?'

'She—that lady—is my wife.'

'Do you mean to tell me that you have actually married this woman, knowing her to be what she herself has represented?'

'Your father seems slow of understanding, Roland. This certificate will assist him, perhaps—show it to him,' said Folly, unfolding the paper given her in the vestry.

'I understand that my son has been tricked into a marriage,' cried Sir Andrew in a fury; 'but if there are laws in England it shall be annulled!'

At the mention of the laws, which she had learned to dread, Folly turned with quick apprehension to Richard Vane.

Coming to her side, he said:

'No one can annul a marriage legally made, as this has been, Sir Andrew. Your son has not been tricked by anyone. You yourself sanctioned his love for the woman who is now his wife; and I, finding that he loved her sincerely, and that she was a good woman and worthy to be the wife of a good man, counselled him to be good also and to marry her.'

'Yes. That's it, sir,' said Roland cheerfully, feeling that the difficulty, thus explained, was half removed. 'I was going to the devil, when Dick came and saved me. He's put the affair just as it is—straightforward and honestly, as he always does. I'm married, and there's no question about——'

'Silence! You are a fool, an idiot!—a mean, base, unworthy scoundrel!' cried the baronet, growing fiercer with each word; 'an unworthy scoundrel, who has respect neither for himself nor his family!—a lying, heartless vagabond!—a—a——'

Sir Andrew shook his stick as he spoke, and at last, unable to find words to express his fury, lifted his stick to strike his son.

Roland crossed his arms and bent his head.

The father's hand fell powerless, and he cried, in a tremulous voice:

'To think that, after all these years of love, you should blast every hope I cherished. You could not do so willingly. I tell you you have been tricked into this marriage for the sake of your money.'

Folly laughed.

'You hear that?' said Sir Andrew. 'The woman's audacious confidence proclaims the fact. Can you believe now that she has married you for love?'

Folly laughed again. Her merriment was more terrible to Roland than his father's anger. He turned and looked at his wife in speechless anxiety to know more.

'Is this not sufficient confirmation for you?' asked Sir Andrew.

Folly looked in her husband's blanched face with cold indifference. He held out his hand to her, and said in an accent of tender supplication:

'Disprove the accusation, Folly.'

She did not move a muscle. After a moment of intense silence, Richard Vane spoke to her.

'Do you not love your husband?' he asked.

'No,' she answered; 'he is too much like his father.'

'I told you so. You have been tricked!' cried Sir Andrew, in bitter exultation. 'And you into the bargain, Richard Vane, in spite of your self-confidence and consummate cleverness. A father's curse be upon you for coming between me and my son—tricked, both of you, by a common mountebank—tricked for your money. But there your scheme shall break down,' said he, addressing Folly for the first time. 'I disown my son —disinherit him. He shall not have another farthing from me—not enough to buy him a crust of bread, though he starve. You have said we are alike—you shall find your words true—for his indifference to my happiness shall be only equalled by my neglect of his. You tell me you were born in a workhouse— may you die there !'

Folly listened, and laughed in a mocking, hard, unmusical tone, as different from her natural sounds of mirth as the voice of a raven from that of a lark.

'You have not married purposelessly,' said Vane, addressing Folly ; ' not purposelessly called us here to witness your own unhappiness—for I conclude it was you who sent for Sir Andrew Aveling ?'

'Yes, I invited him, and he evidently received the letter.'

'Then it will be well to explain your purpose quickly.'

' I am ready. I only wait until Sir Andrew Aveling has done with talking nonsense,' said Folly. 'But perhaps he is satisfied with his own explanation,' she added, with a sneer. 'Perhaps, as he takes all the world to be fools except himself, he classes me with the rest, and thinks it only natural that, wishing to secure his son's fortune, I should take the first opportunity that came of announcing our marriage, and so ruining my own fine prospects in life, eh? Perhaps he will be content to return to the country without any further explanation than that he has suggested, and rest there, satisfied with the hope that his son may die of starvation. If that is the case, I will give him another hope to increase his satisfaction : it is that his son may die of delirium tremens, as assuredly he shall if he be left to my mercy!'

'What does the woman mean?' gasped Sir Andrew.

'What do I mean? This! That I will degrade your son to a lower level than your swine—as I should have degraded him but for the interference which you object to. Had your son carried out the base instructions you gave him, I would have debased him beyond reclaim—by my soul I would! It is well he had a better friend than his father—his punishment is less; and for that you may be grateful to the man you despise —Richard Vane.'

'My God!' exclaimed Sir Andrew, sinking into a chair.

Beads of perspiration stood upon his face.

Roland looked aghast upon his wife.

'I will give you yet another hope to add to the rest. It is that your son may lose the semblance of a man; that all human feeling may depart from him, and that, dying like a dog, he may curse you, his father, for being the cause of all his misery!'

'All his misery!'

'All. For him I have only contempt and pity. He is sacrificed for your sake. Upon him are visited your sins; and the vengeance that God has given into my hands this day falls upon him, that you may suffer. Bare your head, old man, and ask your son to strike you with the cane you lifted against him. Beg him to disown and forget you, for to you he owes all that he suffers and will have to suffer from me. Remorse for the wrong you have done shall follow you to your death-bed, and every compassionate pang that has wrung my poor heart for one I love, shall wring yours for the suffering of the son who was dear to you.'

'I — I will not listen to these idle threats,' stammered Sir Andrew, attempting to rise.

'Idle threats! Leave your son in my power and they shall be proved.' Folly crossed to the door and opened it. 'Go, if you will, fool! It was mercy that induced me to send for you.'

The baronet sank in his chair, paralysed by the terror which Folly's vehement speech and incomprehensible warning produced.'

'What—what have I done?' he faltered.

'Follow me, and you shall see.'

As Folly spoke she passed out of the room.

Sir Andrew rose, collecting his strength by an effort, and passing Roland without a yielding glance, followed Folly.

'Heaven only knows what's going to happen next; stick by us, old man,' murmured Roland to Vane, as they left the room.

CHAPTER XXIV.

SIR ANDREW AVELING AND JOHN MORRISON MEET AGAIN.

OLLY ascended the stairs, and, leading the way through the front bedroom, paused before the door of the room her husband had designed for her special use, until the three gentlemen drew near.

'Remove your hat,' she said to Sir Andrew. The baronet obeyed.

She opened the door and held it as they passed into the room, then she closed it. A screen was extended at a distance of two yards from the door, and the visitors, waiting to be led farther, saw only glimpses of costly furniture and graceful appointments to the right and left.

Folly folded the screen back swiftly, and removed at once any doubt as to what they were brought to see.

In the centre of the beautiful room, under the Venetian glass and surrounded by all the delicate ornaments of the boudoir, stood a plain surgical bedstead. Strapped down to it lay an old man, with his face upwards—an old man with a round, shaven head, on which the veins stood out like blue worms—with a face of which the shrunken skin displayed clearly the frontal and nasal bones of the skull. Deep in the sockets the eyes glittered like stars. His toothless mouth was open, and the folds of his cheeks were contracted with fear.

A stoutly-built young man, in a grey suit, sat upon one of the fancy chairs at the foot of the bed; he rose as Folly removed the screen.

Folly advanced towards the bed.

'I shouldn't go too near him, miss. It'll be on him again before long. He's been watching for nearly an hour, and it's bound to come soon.'

Taking no notice of the caution, Folly leaned over the old man and said:

'Father, father! do you know me?'

He shook his head, and motioned her away impatiently with another movement, still keeping his eyes fixed on one place in the ceiling. The next instant he shrieked out at the highest pitch of his voice, and struggled with every muscle of his body to tear himself from the bed.

'There it is! there it is!' he screamed. 'I knew it was behind there. Let me go—let me go—it is after me—as big as a great bull, and its mouth all black with the blood of my dear babies! Let me go—let me go—it is close upon me—the dead hare——'

The rest of what he cried was incoherent, for he had twisted his head violently backwards, strangling the words and screams as they came from his throat.

'Whoa, ho!' cried the attendant, pressing his brawny hands on the old man's chest, and so bringing the body below the level of the head. 'That's his game to-day,' he said, looking over the old man to the gentlemen with an amused smile. 'Thinks he can break his neck. Last night he was all for killing himself by holding his breath.'

The struggle was of short duration, the old man's strength giving way under his own exertions and the pressure upon his chest.

He shut his eyes; his cries were in a piteous rather than a frantic tone, and came with his breath in short, quick gasps. The young man took advantage of this relapse to tighten up the straps and offer a few words of consolation.

'All right, father, the dead hare's gone, so's the dead babies—all gone running after the gamekeeper—what's-his-name?'

'What, Ledger—little Jim Ledger?' whined the old man.

'Yes, and the squire too.'

'What's he done? Has he stole a dead hare? What's he been hunted for?'

'Why, for sending you to prison for hunting a dead hare.'

'He didn't do me any harm—that shows that you're a liar; you want me to open my eyes and see the dead hare.'

'Bless me, ah, now I come to look it ain't the squire after all—it's—it's——' The clumsy attendant turned to Folly, standing near, and said: 'I've forgot his name—perhaps you can tell me, miss, who it was sent him to prison?'

'Yes, it was that man,' said Folly, pointing to the baronet, 'Sir Andrew Aveling, who sent John Morrison to prison.

'That's the name, that's the name!' cried the old man, catching the words; 'and he killed my wife and took away my babies, and now he hunts me with the dead hare. Liars, liars, liars, it doesn't hunt him! it's him that sets it on to me night and day—night and day.'

Once more John Morrison struggled to break his neck, forcing his chest upwards and his head back until his face grew purple with the strain.

The attendant was upon his chest again, and only the spluttering of the breath through the old man's closed lips broke the silence for a minute.

'He'll be quiet again after this. He couldn't stand it so long if it wasn't for his constitution. He must have been a wonderful fine strong fellow in his time,' the man said.

'You know what sort of a man he was seventeen years ago, when you sent him to prison, Sir Andrew,' said Folly.

The attendant looked up in astonishment. He had conceived that Folly's previous introduction of the baronet's name was merely to sustain his deception.

'I beg your pardon, sir,' he said; 'I didn't

know you was the party who sent him away. I hope no offence.'

The baronet, ashy-pale even to his lips, leaned heavily now upon his son's arm.

'Let me go away from this frightful scene,' he said hoarsely.

'It's all right now, sir,' said the attendant. 'He's exhausted now. Though his eyes are open he is dead asleep, if you'd like to look at him.'

'Yes, come and see your work,' said Folly; 'the man you sent to gaol is your son's father now. You may be more ready to resign your son if you see the state to which he may be brought. Come, look at him and see the traces of the manhood you have destroyed—look at this poor, poor face.' She bent over the head of the bed, taking her father's hideous face between her hands as she spoke. 'Look at these eyes that have wept away their tenderness—this brow that covers a distracted brain—this body that outlives its broken heart—look at this old, old man of fifty years, whose closing days are unblessed with sweet repose and visions of welcoming heavenly angels, who living is racked by the torments of an unmerited hell. See this wretched body, and prepare to answer Heaven for the soul you have torn from it. Look at us—your kin—your son's bride and father.'

With these words she threw herself upon the bed beside John Morrison, and, burying her face in his shoulder, burst into an awful peal of laughter.

END OF VOL. II.

BENTLEYS' EMPIRE LIBRARY.

The following Volumes can be obtained separately at every Bookseller's price 2s. 6d. each.

I.
By HELEN MATHERS.
THE LAND O' THE LEAL.

II.
By FLORENCE MONTGOMERY.
A VERY SIMPLE STORY, and, *WILD MIKE.*

III.
By Mrs. ALEXANDER.
RALPH WILTON'S WEIRD.

IV.
By Mrs. ANNIE EDWARDES.
A BLUE STOCKING.

V.
By HELEN MATHERS.
AS HE COMES UP THE STAIR.

VI.
ANONYMOUS.
FIVE YEARS' PENAL SERVITUDE.

VII.
By WILKIE COLLINS.
A ROGUE'S LIFE.

VIII.
By A GERMAN PRIEST.
A VICTIM OF THE FALK LAWS.

IX.
By Mrs. ANNIE EDWARDES.
A VAGABOND HEROINE.

X.
By Mrs. G. W. GODFREY.
MY QUEEN.

XI.
By JULIAN HAWTHORNE.
ARCHIBALD MALMAISON.

XII.
By RHODA BROUGHTON.
TWILIGHT STORIES.

XIII.
By CHARLES DICKENS.
THE MUDFOG PAPERS. (*Now first republished.*)

XIV.
By FLORENCE MONTGOMERY.
HERBERT MANNERS, and other *STORIES.*

OTHER VOLUMES ARE IN PREPARATION.

LONDON:
RICHARD BENTLEY & SON, NEW BURLINGTON STREET.

OR,
Mirth and Marvels.

"Abundant in humour, observation, fancy; in extensive knowledge of books and men; in palpable hits of character, exquisite grave irony, and the most whimsical indulgence in point of epigram. We cannot open a page that is not sparkling with its wit and humour, that is not ringing with its strokes of pleasantry and satire."--*Examiner.*

I.
The "Victoria" Edition.
A Pocket Edition, in fcap. 8vo., with Frontispiece, 2s., cloth.

II.
The Popular Edition.
In crown 8vo., 3s. 6d., cloth.

III.
The Edinburgh Edition.
An entirely new Edition, in large type, with Thirty-two Illustrations by CRUIKSHANK, LEECH, TENNIEL, and DU MAURIER, especially Re-engraved for this Edition by Mr. GEORGE PEARSON. In crown 8vo., 6s., red cloth; also bound in golden cloth, paper label, same price.

IV.
The Carmine Edition.
In large crown 8vo. With a carmine border line around each page. Seventeen Illustrations by CRUIKSHANK and LEECH, Gilt edges and bevelled boards, 10s. 6d.

V.
The Burlington Edition.
A Cabinet Edition, in 3 vols., fcap. 8vo., 10s. 6d.

VI.
The Illustrated Edition.
With Sixty Illustrations by CRUIKSHANK, LEECH, and TENNIEL; and cover designed by JOHN LEIGHTON, F.S.A. Crown 4to., cloth, bevelled boards, gilt edges, 21s. The same Edition, bound in the Ely pattern, 21s.; or in WHITE cloth, Ely pattern (for presentation), 22s. 6d.
"A series of humorous legends, illustrated by three such men as CRUIKSHANK, LEECH, and TENNIEL—what can be more tempting?"—*Times.*

VII.
The Annotated Edition.
A Library Edition, with a History of each Legend, and other Notes, and some original Legends now first published. Edited by the Rev. RICHARD DALTON BARHAM. In 2 vols., demy 8vo., with an original Frontispiece by GEORGE CRUIKSHANK; and all the Illustrations by CRUIKSHANK and LEECH. 24s.

To be obtained at every Bookseller's.

LONDON:
RICHARD BENTLEY & SON, NEW BURLINGTON STREET.

www.ingramcontent.com/pod-product-compliance
Lightning Source LLC
Chambersburg PA
CBHW032049230426
43672CB00009B/1534